# Successful Student Writing Through Formative Assessment

Harry Grover Tuttle, Ed.D.

Routledge
Taylor & Francis Group
LONDON AND NEW YORK

First published 2010 by Eye On Education

Published 2013 by Routledge
711 Third Avenue, New York, NY 10017, USA
2 Park Square, Milton Park, Abingdon, Oxon OX14 4RN

*Routledge is an imprint of the Taylor & Francis Group, an informa business*



A sincere effort has been made to supply the identity of those who have created specific strategies. Any omissions have been unintentional.

Notices
No responsibility is assumed by the publisher for any injury and/or damage to persons or property as a matter of products liability, negligence or otherwise, or from any use of operation of any methods, products, instructions or ideas contained in the material herein.

Practitioners and researchers must always rely on their own experience and knowledge in evaluating and using any information, methods, compounds, or experiments described herein. In using such information or methods they should be mindful of their own safety and the safety of others, including parties for whom they have a professional responsibility.

Product or corporate names may be trademarks or registered trademarks, and are used only for identification and explanation without intent to infringe.

**Library of Congress Cataloging-in-Publication Data**
Tuttle, Harry Grover.
Successful student writing through formative assessment / Harry Grover Tuttle.
p. cm.
Includes bibliographical references.
ISBN 978-1-59667-128-7
1. English language—Composition and exercises—Study and teaching (Middle school) 2. English language—Composition and exercises—Study and teaching (Secondary) 3. Curriculum-based assessment. I. Title.
LB1631.T88 2009
808'.0420712—dc22

2009023803

ISBN-13: 978-1-596-67128-7 (pbk)

## *Also Available from EYE ON EDUCATION*

**Formative Assessment: Responding to Your Students**
Harry Grover Tuttle

**Empowering Students to Write and Re-Write: Standards-Based Strategies for Middle and High School Teachers**
Warren E. Combs

**Writing in the Content Areas, 2nd Edition**
Amy Benjamin

**Writing Put to the Test: Teaching for the High Stakes Essay**
Amy Benjamin

**Vocabulary at the Center**
Amy Benjamin and John T. Crow

**Formative Assessment for English Language Arts: A Guide for Middle and High School Teachers**
Amy Benjamin

**Differentiating Assessment in Middle and High School English and Social Studies**
Sheryn Spencer Waterman

**Motivating Every Student in Literacy (Including the Highly Unmotivated!) Grades 3–6**
Sandra K. Athans and Denise Ashe Devine

**Literacy Leadership Teams: Collaborative Leadership for Improving and Sustaining Student Achievement**
Pamela S. Craig

**Differentiated Assessment for Middle and High School Classrooms**
Deborah Blaz

**Teacher-Made Assessments: How to Connect Curriculum, Instruction, and Student Learning**
Christopher Gareis and Leslie Grant

**Rigor is NOT A Four-Letter Word**
Barbara R. Blackburn

**Short Cycle Assessment: Improving Student Achievement Through Formative Assessment**
Susan Lang, Todd Stanley and Betsy Moore

# Free Downloads

Many of the tools discussed and displayed in this book are also available on the Routledge website as Adobe Acrobat files. Permission has been granted to purchasers of this book to download these tools and print them.

You can access these downloads by visiting www.routledge.com/9781596671287 and clicking on the Free Downloads tab.

# About the Author

**Dr. Harry Grover Tuttle** has taught English writing courses in high schools and colleges to people whose native language is English and not English, both in the United States and in Latin America. For numerous years, Dr. Tuttle edited both an international journal for the International Society for Technology in Education (ISTE) and a state journal for the New York State Association of Technology in Education.

For the past few years, Dr. Tuttle has written formative assessment articles for Grant Wiggins' Big Idea website. In addition, he has been a technology integration teacher and a technology coordinator for a city district. He also served as president of ISTE's technology coordinators' SIG and of the New York State Association for Computers and Technology in Education. He is the author of four books. His last book, *Formative Assessment: Responding to Your Students*, presents a step-by-step approach to implementing formative assessment in your classroom. Dr. Tuttle focuses on assessing and improving student learning, and he speaks internationally and consults with schools. He enjoys sharing with teachers new avenues of learning through his blog, *http://www.eduwithtechn.wordpress.com*, where he frequently writes about formative assessment.

# Contents

# Preface

This book is based on the English writing courses that I have taught in school and in colleges to both people whose native language is English and whose first language is not English. I wish to thank my students for what they have taught me about the effectiveness of formative assessment in their own writing. Their honest feedback through class comments, reflections, and writings have helped me to understand what works and what does not work for them. With their help, I have learned to become better at monitoring, diagnosing, giving feedback, and building in time for them to improve. I have learned to take time to celebrate their writing mini-successes and to celebrate their drastic growth in writing. I wish to thank the students who have given me permission to share their thoughts and their work in this publication.

I now teach at the college level and use these formative assessments in the beginning writing courses where numerous students are working on their G.E.D. I know from my past school experience that these ideas will work with students from middle school to high school.

As I have implemented formative assessments in my writing classroom, I have come to understand how critical it is for students to receive immediate feedback on each part of their writing. The sooner they find out that they have a learning gap, the sooner they, another student, or I can help them to improve. As their writing is monitored, diagnosed, and given feedback, they move from learning gaps to learning strengths; they move from many small wins to a cumulative big win in their writing.

I appreciate the assistance of Robert Doolittle, Melody Mariani, and Joellyn Tuttle who peer-reviewed the chapters.

In addition, I wish to thank Robert Sickles and Jennifer Lee, my editors.

This book is dedicated to my grandson, Rowan James Tuttle, and future grandchildren so that their teachers can use formative assessment to help them become good communicators through writing.

# Introduction

I wonder why we humans have been teaching writing for thousands of years, and yet we do not have it perfected. Even students who graduate from high school still have difficulty in writing paragraphs and essays, and college freshman English students attest to their problems in writing.

Formative assessment focuses on improving students' writing. Because continuous growth is an important aspect of formative assessment, your students will grow in their writing during each part of the writing process (Ainsworth & Viegut, 2007). They do not wait for the revision phase of the writing process to improve their work. Likewise, according to formative assessment, each piece of your students' writing will show improvement over the previous writing. As you go through the formative assessment steps of identifying the writing standards, observing the students' writing, diagnosing their learning strengths and learning gaps, providing formative feedback to them, and giving them time to improve, you assist your students in moving from being struggling writers to proficient writers.

This book takes formative assessment theory and transforms it into practice for your writing classroom. The activities in this book are activities that have enabled students to show drastic improvements in their writing. The writing statements and samples are from real students.

As teachers of students from middle school through college, you can use these various techniques to help your students move forward in their writing. You can use these techniques with very little, if any, modification.

Although there are many formats for essays, I have chosen to use the five-paragraph format throughout the book for consistency. The classic five-paragraph format allows students to organize and develop an idea that is supported in a logical and well-developed manner. This most commonly used in-class writing format provides a solid scaffold for writers who display writing learning gaps. Once your students have mastered this format, they can transfer their skills to other essay formats.

The book has two major sections: The *Formative Assessment Overview* section provides a theoretical introductory overview of formative assessment with explanations and examples of monitoring, diagnosing, giving feedback, and providing time to grow. It also includes a section on grading within formative assessment.

The *Formative Assessments for Writing* section incorporates the theory of the formative assessment into a multitude of actual formative assessments for prewriting, writing, and revising. If you are familiar with formative assessment theory, you can instantly go to this section for the specifics on using it in your classroom section.

I am confident that as you implement these formative assessment techniques, you will notice the drastic difference in your students' writing. You will not have to wait until the end of the year to see improvement; you will see a dramatic change from their first writing to the next.

# Section I

# Formative Assessment Overview

How do you help students to become better writers? Writing more without improving each time is like practicing the same wrong notes in a piano piece. The end result is that students can more easily make mistakes. Our goal is student improvement in writing. Formative assessment incorporates monitoring, diagnosing, and providing feedback for students' continual success.

Imagine if your car makes a horrible, loud noise and you do not know what is wrong. You take it to a mechanic. The mechanic listens to the car, looks under the hood, and drives it. If he says, "You've got a serious problem. Leave!" you will be very upset. You want to know what is wrong and how it can be fixed. Unfortunately, this mechanic metaphor is what happens in many writing classrooms. Students receive a grade on a paper after they have gone through the writing process. The grade does not help the students to understand specifically what they can do to improve. Most of the traditional English composition shortcut comments on students' papers such as "AWK" for "awkward" do not tell the students how to improve. The writers are left with their broken writing. They want their mechanic (you) to help them become better writers.

Formative assessment can be defined as the continual growth cycle of monitoring, diagnosing, giving feedback, allowing time for growth, and affirming growth (Tuttle, 2009). Formative assessment can be compared to a doctor's visit. At the doctor's office, a nurse takes your vital signs (monitors you). The doctor asks you some additional questions or examines you (monitors you). Then the doctor compares your present condition to a healthy condition to determine your medical condition (diagnosis for achievement) and then decides what strategy will help you to improve (diagnosis for strategy). Next, this doctor informs you of your condition and the strategy for improvement in such a way that you will understand your condition and will want to use that strategy (feedback). You take the medicine for the designated time (the specific feedback strategy for improvement), so that your body can improve (time for growth). You feel healthy again (reporting growth). The figure below illustrates the stages of formative assessment as applied to writing.

**Formative Assessment Stages**

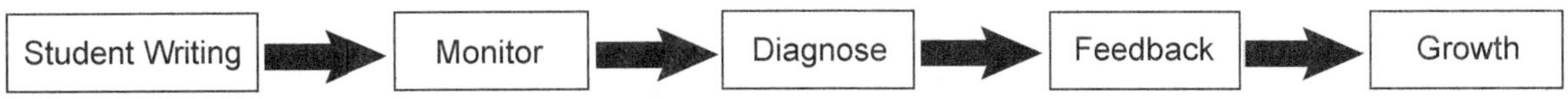


Just as the doctor's office visit is a seamless process, the formative assessment process in the classroom becomes a natural part of the classroom. By modifying what you already do, you can implement the formative assessment process for improved student writing.

Formative assessment transforms the writing process. In formative assessment, students are monitored, diagnosed, and given feedback through each part of each step of the writing process. For example, during the prewriting phase, students, peers, or you review the students' narrowed topic, thesis, idea generation, and idea organization (see figure below). In contrast, the traditional assessment process starts at the revision stage, which occurs three quarters of the way through the writing process, after the students have already completed the prewriting and the draft phase. Formative assessments need to start earlier if students are to produce high-quality writing. Their early ideas are like cement that quickly hardens unless you can modify those ideas very early in the process (Hunter, 1976). Likewise, after students start building their writing, they do not want to tear down any of their construction. Formative assessment begins as soon as students have an idea for a building, not after they have built it. Assessments are built in to guarantee success at each step. Therefore, formative assessment basically adds the "revision" part of the writing process into each part of the process. When students arrive at the formal revision stage, their work has already been assessed many times; they make fewer changes as they move through the writing process. Usually their transition from the draft to the published version involves minimal changes since they have already improved their paper through the other stages.

**Formative Assessments in the Writing Process**

| Writing Process | Formative Assessment On |
|---|---|
| Prewriting | Narrowed Topic<br>Thesis statement<br>Idea generation<br>Idea organization |
| Writing | Paragraph and Essay structure/Formula<br>Topic sentence<br>Evidence<br>Detailed examples<br>Sequence – transitions<br>Vocabulary<br>Sentence variety<br>Introductory paragraph<br>Concluding paragraph |
| Revising | "I can" statements<br>Checklists<br>Essay Improvement |

In addition, formative assessments build on many small writing assessments so that young writers can experience many small wins. Their small wins contribute to their confidence as a writer. They know if they have a learning gap that they will be instantly given formative feedback to redirect their writing to be successful. They go from having a learning gap to a learning strength (a mini-win).

Formative assessment plays a key role in Response to Intervention (RTI) in which teachers instruct, monitor, diagnose, and give feedback so students can improve on essential skills (Howell, Patton, & Deiotte, 2008). In RTI, Tier 1 Intervention, the classroom basic intervention, is sufficient for 80 to 90% of the students. Classroom teachers such as yourself look for red flags that show lack of achievement (monitor the students), intervene with a new strategy or a modification of an existing strategy (diagnosis and feedback), and reassess students. If students do not show growth after numerous tries, another strategy or modification is used. If the students still do not show progress, they move to Tier 2 Intervention and, if necessary, to Tier 3 Intervention. The formative assessment idea of helping students succeed at critical skills is vital to RTI, as is the idea that students need immediate intervention to be able to grow.

# 1

# Writing Prerequisites

Before you begin to apply the formative assessment process to your students' writing, it is helpful to think through some prerequisites. First, you might want to understand what the writing standards are; most state standards refer to writing very generally, such as "writing for information and personal expression." Without a specific understanding of the final writing learning goals you expect of your students, you cannot consistently be measuring them against this end. Also, you can determine how you will assess these writing standards so that you can focus your instruction and feedback on helping students to be successful on this particular manner of demonstrating the standards. As you constantly assess your students, you can make sure that not only are they learning the writing standards, but that they are learning these standards with a high degree of skill. To meet the last prerequisite, you can gather exemplary material that represents these standards and your high expectations for the standards and share these exemplars with your students.

This chapter contains information on these sections:

- Standards
- Assessment
- Exemplars

## Standards

In formative assessment, the three major critical questions are as follows: What is the end learning goal for the students? Where are the students in the process at present? What can be done to help the learners move forward?

Before you can plan your writing instruction, you will want to understand what the general writing standards really mean (Figure 1.1). Your initial reaction to these vague concepts may be to ask for the writing final exam since the final usually shows what is important in a class. However, there is no one uniform writing final because each teacher often creates his/her own. Therefore, there is no uniform school expectation for the course. The district or school may not have clarified the writing standards, and students may "be able to do" vastly different things based on their individual teacher.

**Figure 1.1. Course Writing Standard to Specific Learning Goal**

What do these writing standards signify in practical terms? For the students, the purpose of writing can be boiled down to "to write paragraphs and essays" or "to write essays and a research report." With that singular focus in class, you can help the learners improve in writing essays and research papers.

Your decisions about your students' writing will help you focus more clearly on the precise expectations for the students, on the formative assessments to measure their progress, and how you can help them be successful writers. Think through some of the following writing questions (Figure 1.2).

**Figure 1.2. Writing Questions and Possible Answers**

| Question About Writing | Possible Answer |
|---|---|
| Which writing standards will the pupils use? | Information |
| Will they do literary, academic, or both types of writing? | Academic |
| Which academic writing types will they use? | Argument, Compare/Contrast, Definition/Classification, Illustration, Process/How-to, and Research Paper |
| What type essay format will the writers use? | Five paragraph: introduction, three body paragraphs, and conclusion |
| For any writing type, which format will the learners use?<br>For compare and contrast writing, will the students only compare, only contrast or do both in the same essay? | Contrast |
| For a contrast essay, will students write topical (all the differences for one topic, then all the differences for the other topic) or point by point (contrast each item for both topics in the same paragraph)? | Point by Point |
| How many categories of differences will the writers use? | Three or more |
| How many points will they have for each category? | Three |
| How specific do the points have to be? | Very detailed such as numbers, names of places, or the specific day |

Another critical issue in formative assessment is what constitutes "good" or proficient writing. Again, your district or school may not have a model or exemplar for its teachers. Each teacher creates his or her own idea of a "proficient" paper. Therefore, there is a great variety in what is considered proficient writing in the school. This level of quality has to be determined. You may develop a rubric that explains your expectations for a well-written paper (see *Assessment* below).

Unless there is a central file or depository (physical or virtual) of other instructors' thinking and material, you will reinvent the wheel and decide on specific writing standards for the course, create your own expectations for each standard, make up your own assessments, and create your own lesson plans. Unlike Isaac Newton who stood "on the shoulders of giants" (built on the work of those who came before him), you are left to dig your own education writing trench. One technique is to work with a writing team from your school or a virtual team who can jointly make these decisions, pool resources, pool their expertise, examine students' work together, and create alternative activities that directly assist the students to become better writers. If you do not have a team, you can begin to collect your own resources based on previous writing units you have taught, to focus on helping students be better writers.

## Assessment

In preparing for formative assessment in your writing class, you have defined the writing standards. Now you can decide how you will assess the students' work. Without a precise understanding of the way in which you will assess the students, you do not know how to structure your instruction and the materials to guide your students to be proficient writers. You will develop a formative assessment rubric to assess the students' writing.

Most writing rubrics, including those found on the Internet, do not identify the specific characteristics needed for being proficient. When students read terms like "purposeful," "focus," "strong beginning," and "varied sentence structure," they often feel like they are looking through a fog. These words are vague abstract terms for the writers. The vast majority of the rubrics are written in teacher educational jargon as opposed to student-friendly language.

In addition, these online rubrics are summative; their purpose is to give students a grade. When students see a checked item (a learning gap or an area for improvement) on the rubric, they usually only see a general area for improvement such as "Development." The students may not be able to identify the specific learning gap in that general area, such as "sequencing." These summative rubrics do not contain useful suggestions to help the students overcome the learning gap. If the students already knew how to interpret the term "strong voice" to improve their writing, they would do so.

You may rewrite a persuasion rubric from Rubistar (http://rubistar.4teachers.org/index.php?screen=CustomizeTemplate&bank_rubric_id=127&section_id=5&) into a general writing rubric to enable students see the specific strengths and weaknesses of their writing. To avoid the very general five or six categories found in most rubrics, this new rubric includes eleven distinct categories (prewriting, five paragraphs, topic sentences, evidence and details, specific essay type, sequencing and transitions, conclusion, vocabulary and voice, mechanics, and revision after peer review). Students will be able to see their individual strengths; they will be able to see specific areas for improvements. This rubric fits on one page both sides (Figures 1.4 and 1.5, page 12).

Can the students understand the rubric well enough to know what they have to do to improve if they receive a less than proficient score? Is the rubric worded in a language that the students can understand? The students read this new rubric over carefully. If they find any word or phrase that they do not completely understand, they circle it. They know that you will use this rubric to assess them so they need to understand fully what they are being evaluated on. All students finish in about four minutes and they hand the rubric back in. When you look over their papers, you notice that more than one quarter of the students have circled words such as "detailed" or "attention getter," so you rewrite the rubric by paraphrasing the terms.

The morning before passing out the new version of the rubric, you have the epiphany that there are not any specific examples in the rubric. This scoring tool tells the students what good writing is, but does not show examples of the writing. The present rubric has fallen into the "telling, not showing" gap that many students demonstrate in their writing. So, you add an example in the "above proficient" column for each category. For example, in the "evidence" category, for the thesis of "Americans are obsessed with spending money," the specific evidence of "cell phones" is added.

Now that the students comprehend the level of writing that the rubric requires, they use it to evaluate a short essay. Once more they circle any word or phrase that they do not understand in the rubric as they apply it to actual writing. Some learners still want more clarification of the terms in the rubric, so you revise the rubric again to make the terms clearer.

Now you can explain to these writers how you will use this rubric to assess their writing. Tell them you will put a plus sign (+) next to the words/terms that indicate their strengths, and that you will underline the words/terms that indicate their learning gaps. If you underline a learning gap from the rubric, then you will circle the good example from the "Above Proficient" column to illustrate what a good example looks like. In addition, you let them know that you will limit your rubric feedback to a few critical areas. You will expect that they will improve from one writing to the next.

# Figure 1.4. English Essay Rubric, Side 1

Name: Date: Essay type:

| | Above Proficient | Proficient | Developing | Beginning |
|---|---|---|---|---|
| **Preorganization (outline, concept map, web, listing, etc.)** | Author shows a completed detailed prewriting organization that includes thesis, each paragraph's topic, three pieces of evidence and three details for each piece of evidence | Author shows an almost completed detailed prewriting organization. | Author shows a vague writing organization which lacks topics, evidence or details. | Author does not have a completed detailed prewriting organization. |
| **5-Paragraph Format** | Has clearly defined introductory paragraph, three body paragraphs, and a concluding paragraph. | Has introductory paragraph, three body paragraphs, and a concluding paragraph. | Has four paragraphs. | Has less than four paragraphs or each paragraph's purpose is unclear. |
| **Introductory Paragraph Attention Grabber and Thesis** | The introductory paragraph has a one- to two-sentence attention grabber such as a startling statement, a relevant quotation, statistic, or question addressed to the reader. For the thesis of "Americans are obsessed with spending money," an attention grabber is "Money makes the world go around and that spinning causes an obsession."<br>The thesis statement directly states the topic of the essay and provides a clear, strong statement of the author's position on the topic in one sentence. It is the last statement in the introductory paragraph. Example: "Americans are obsessed with spending money (Americans = topic; are obsessed with spending money = position).<br>The introductory paragraph only contains the short attention grabber and the thesis, two to three sentences. | The introductory paragraph has an attention grabber although it is not focused tightly on the thesis.<br>The thesis statement states the topic of the essay and provides a clear, strong statement of the author's position on the topic. It is the last statement in the introductory paragraph.<br>The paragraph only contains the attention grabber and the thesis. | The author has an attention grabber that does not relate to the thesis.<br>The thesis statement states the topic of the essay in a general manner or it does not show the author's position on the topic.<br>The thesis is not the last sentence in the introductory paragraph.<br>The paragraph contains other unnecessary sentences. | There is no attention grabber in the introductory paragraph.<br>The thesis statement does not state the topic of the essay and has no statement of the author's position on the topic.<br>The paragraph contains many unnecessary sentences. |
| **For each of the three body paragraphs: Topic sentences support the thesis** | Each paragraph starts with a topic sentence that clearly shows how that topic supports the thesis. For the money obsession thesis, a topic sentence may be "Americans' craziness over money shows in their technology purchases." | All paragraphs start with a topic sentence that shows how that topic supports the thesis. | Two paragraphs start with a topic sentence supporting the thesis. | One or no paragraph starts with a topic sentence supporting the thesis. |
| **For each of the three body paragraphs: Evidence to prove the thesis and Details to support the evidence** | Each paragraph includes three or more pieces of evidence (general categories) that support the thesis and supporting specific details (one to three concrete specific details (facts, statistics, examples, real-life experiences). Each paragraph is fully developed; it does not include any unnecessary (off topic) information. For the money obsession thesis, an evidence is cell phones and another is TVs.<br>A detail is "Americans do not buy basic cells, they buy high-end Internet/TV-ready ones such as the LG VU." | Each paragraph includes three or more pieces of evidence. Each piece of evidence has three examples. Each paragraph is developed and it may include one piece of unnecessary information.<br>Almost all the details are specific (not an expensive shoe but a $170 Steve Madden high heel shoe) and support the thesis. | The paragraph includes two pieces of evidence that support the topic sentence. Each evidence has two examples.<br>Each paragraph has some developed and contains two pieces of unnecessary information.<br>More than three quarters of the details are specific and support the thesis; there are two details per evidence. | The paragraph includes one or fewer pieces of evidence.<br>Each paragraph lacks development and contains more than two pieces of unnecessary information.<br>The details are neither relevant nor specific. There are very few details. |
| **Specific essay type such as Compare–Contrast, Cause–Effect, Classification, Argument, Illustration, and Research** | The author includes all the essential characteristics for that type of writing such as demonstrating how two things are similar in a comparison paper. | The author meets the criteria that makes it that type of writing. | The author generally meets most of the criteria that makes it that type of writing. | The author does not meet the criteria that makes it that type of writing. |

# Figure 1.5. English Essay Rubric, Side 2

| | Above Proficient | Proficient | Developing | Beginning |
|---|---|---|---|---|
| **Sequencing (organization among paragraphs and within paragraphs) and Transitions (connecting paragraphs and connecting sentences within a paragraph)** | Paragraphs and sentences within each paragraph are logically ordered (by time sequence: on Wednesday; by location: on the left; or by emphasis: the most important) to make it easy to follow the author's ideas. Example: birth to first year; back of the car to its front; and the worst job to the best.<br>The author uses a variety of thoughtful transitions such as "next," "also," "on Friday," and "at three o'clock." These transitions clearly show how the ideas are connected among paragraphs and within paragraphs. "Also, they buy expensive clothing such as Coach and Louis Vitton." | Paragraphs are logically ordered. The evidence, examples and details, are provided in a fairly logical order that makes it reasonably easy to follow the author's ideas.<br>The author uses many transitions and has much variety in transitions. Almost always transitions clearly show how the ideas are connected among paragraphs and within paragraphs. | Paragraphs are mostly ordered.<br>A few of the evidence, examples and details, is not in an expected or logical order, distracting the reader and making the essay seem a little confusing.<br>The author uses several transitions or has a little variety in transitions. Sometimes transitions clearly show how the ideas are connected among paragraphs and within paragraphs. | Paragraphs lack an order.<br>Many of the support evidence, examples and details are not in an expected or logical order. They distract the reader and make the essay seem very confusing.<br>The transitions among ideas are unclear or do not exist. |
| **Concluding paragraph—thesis and extender (expander) of the thesis** | The concluding paragraph clearly restates the thesis in one sentence and then thoughtfully extends the idea in the next sentence. Example: "Americans reveal their obsession for spending in buying expensive technology, clothing, and homes. Hopefully, their huge bills will not bankrupt them so that instead of living in a $600,000 home, they end up living in a tent as a homeless person." There are no other sentences. | The concluding paragraph restates the thesis and extends the idea. This paragraph does not include other sentences. | The concluding paragraph does not restates the thesis. It does not extend the idea. The concluding paragraph contains other unnecessary sentences. | There is no concluding paragraph; the paper just ends after the last paragraph. |
| Vocabulary and Voice | The author consistently uses precise words that vividly support the thesis and expresses voice (your personality). Examples for the money obsession thesis: "They spend over one hundred dollars a week to fill up their expensive cars such as a Hummer or Ford Expedition."<br>The author uses synonyms for the key thesis words. "War" becomes "battle" or "conflict." | The author generally uses precise words that vividly support the thesis and expresses his/her voice in almost all of the writing.<br>The author generally three or more synonyms for the thesis. | The author often uses precise words that vividly support the thesis and expresses voice in some parts of the writing.<br>The author uses one to two synonyms for the thesis. | The author rarely uses precise words that vividly support the thesis. The author does not use voice in any consistent manner.<br>The author does not use any synonyms for the key thesis words. |
| **Sentence structure, mechanics, grammar, spelling, capitalization, or punctuation** | All sentences are well-constructed with varied structure (short sentences, long ones, and different sentence beginnings).<br>Avoids "You" or "I's" in the essay.<br>Avoids "is" or "are."<br>Does not start a sentence with "This is," "It," or "And."<br>Author makes no errors in grammar, spelling, capitalization, punctuation, or sentence structure that distract the reader from the content.<br>Does not switch from "You" to "I " or "they." | Most sentences are well-constructed and there is some varied sentence structure in the essay.<br>Usually avoids "You" or "I's" in the essay.<br>Avoids "is" or "are."<br>Does not usually start a sentence with "This is," "It" , or "And."<br>Author makes one to two errors in grammar, spelling, capitalization, punctuation, or sentence structure that distract the reader from the content.<br>Does not switch from "You" to "I" or "they." | Most sentences are well constructed; there is no variation is structure.<br>Sometimes avoids "You" or "I's" in the essay. Often uses "is" or "are."<br>Sometimes starts a sentence with "This is," "It,", or "And."<br>Author makes three to four errors in grammar, spelling, capitalization, punctuation, or sentence structure that distract the reader from the content.<br>Sometimes switches from "You" to "I" or "they." | Most sentences are not well-constructed nor varied.<br>Uses "You" or "I's" throughout the essay.<br>Consistently uses "is" or "are."<br>Often starts a sentence with "This is," "It," or "And."<br>Author makes five or more errors in grammar, spelling, capitalization, punctuation, or sentence structure that distract the reader from the content.<br>Often switches from "You" to "I" or "they." |
| **Revisions after peer, self, or teacher assessment** | Author demonstrates very thoughtful and thorough revisions that greatly improve the essay. | Author demonstrates thoughtful and mostly thorough revisions that improve the most critical parts of the essay. | Author demonstrates many revisions that improve numerous critical parts of the essay. | Author demonstrates few revisions or the revisions do not make any major improvements in the essay. |

Peer's or Teacher's specific suggestions for improvement:

1

2

3

Rating __________

## Exemplars

What happens when you look at your students' writing, and you realize that they do not understand your expectations for the particular essay? In addition to determining the exact standard and ascertaining the assessment of the writing, students need to see other students' exemplary writing so that they better understand the type of writing and the high quality of writing that is expected of them (Figure 1.6).

**Figure 1.6. An Exemplar Changes Students' Writing**

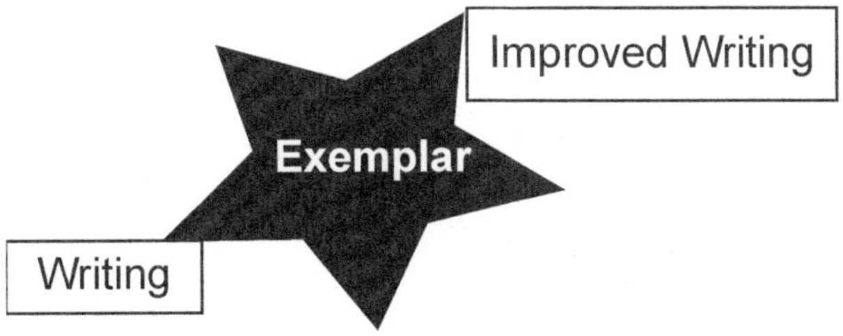


Likewise, when the struggling students read "exemplary" literary examples such as those often found in textbooks, they usually get lost in the literary examples. Usually these passages are packed with words your students do not know, are written in such a sophisticated manner that the students cannot find the key writing elements, and are written so well that the students are overwhelmed ("I cannot write that well!). In addition, literary passages often intertwine different types of writing patterns so that the students cannot easily identify the one specific pattern of writing.

If your colleagues do not have a collection of exemplars for the various types of writing, you need to find or create some writing exemplars and then help your students understand what makes your exemplar so good in terms of the standard. You can look through a pile of papers from last year's students and find a few solid samples of student work there. Even if they are not exemplary, you can modify them to become an exemplar.

Your goal is to help students understand why a writing example is an exemplar. After the students read an exemplary passage (Figure 1.7, page 14), help them analyze it. Create a blank graphic organizer on the board or show them one made in the Inspiration computer program, a visual learning tool that allows the user to easily and quickly create a graphic organizer. You ask them what is the topic for the classification and they identify "desserts." Next you ask them to identify the three classifications of desserts. Write the three classifications in the second, third, and fourth columns of the second row of the graphic organizer. Ask your students what the characteristics of each category are as you put these in the left column going down. Then ask them to copy the graphic organizer (Figure 1.8, page 14) and complete the detail for each characteristic for each category (Figure 1.9, page 15).

### Figure 1.7. Classification Exemplar

When people hear "It's time for dessert," they smile. People look forward to delicious after-dinner treats. Their desserts can be classified as baked goods, dairy, or fruit. A baked good, such as a pumpkin pie, makes up the first category of desserts. People bake homemade pies in their kitchen. As soon as it comes out of the oven, they serve this warm homemade dessert. They eat it with a fork. Although pumpkin pie tastes delicious, it only has medium nutritional value. A second type of dessert consists of dairy, such as chocolate chip ice cream. An ice cream factory produces frozen food. People eat this very cold food with a spoon. Even though ice cream has a wonderful taste, it has very little nutritional value. The last class of desserts consists of fruit, such as an Empire apple. Orchards produce these apples. People eat them at room temperature by holding the apples in their hands. As they crunch into this fruit, they obtain high nutrition from eating apples.

### Figure 1.8. Empty Classification Chart

| Classification: Dessert | | | |
|---|---|---|---|
| | **Baked Goods** | **Dairy** | **Fruit** |
| Example | | | |
| Characteristics | | | |
| Where made | | | |
| Temperature | | | |
| Tool | | | |
| Nutrition | | | |

**Figure 1.9. Completed Classification Chart**

| Classification: Dessert | | | |
|---|---|---|---|
| | **Baked Goods** | **Dairy** | **Fruit** |
| Example | Pumpkin pie | Chocolate chip ice cream | Empire apple |
| Characteristics | | | |
| Where made | Home made | Ice cream factory | Orchard |
| Temperature | Warm | Cold | Room temperature |
| Tool | Fork | Spoon | Hand |
| Nutrition | Medium | Low | High |

After the pupils have completed the graphic organizer, ask them how sure they are of the differences among the three classifications of a dessert. Show them how you completed the graphic organizer so they can compare their results to yours. All students believe they are 100% sure of the differences among the classifications. They realize that these classification categories have to be very distinct; likewise, the examples of each have to be very specific. In their writing, they are to make sure that the classifications are as clear as the ones for dessert writing.

Sometimes you give your students an exemplar (Figure 1.10, page 16), ask them to read it, and explain to them why it is an exemplar. As an alternative, you can give them two exemplar essays, such as two classification essays, for them to analyze the pattern of writing.

## Figure 1.10. Exemplar Contrast Essay

### Grocery Stores

Martha's son, Fred, only eats meat and potatoes whereas her daughter, Ana, avoids meat. How does a person decide where to buy food for her family? Does she go to the supermarket or to a neighborhood store? A neighborhood grocery store differs greatly from a supermarket grocery store in terms of prices, appearance, and employees.

The neighborhood grocery store charges more for products than the supermarket. White bread costs $2.00 a loaf at the neighborhood store while at the supermarket the same bread only costs $1.25. Likewise, milk weighs in at $4.75 at the neighborhood store; however, at the supermarket that same gallon of milk costs just $3.75. Also, although a fifteen-ounce box of cereal costs $4.00 at the neighborhood store, an eighteen-ounce box of the same cereal has the lower price of $3.25 at the bigger store. At the neighborhood store a person pays $10.75 for these three items, whereas these same three items only cost $8.25 at the supermarket.

The neighborhood store has a negative appearance when compared to the supermarket. The windows are covered with grime in the neighborhood store. In contrast, the supermarket has sparkling clean windows. Similarly, electrical wires hang out of holes in the walls in the neighborhood store. Yet, the supermarket does not have any holes; it has attractive pictures. Next, the floor of the neighborhood grocery store has many tiles missing so that a person has difficulty walking on the floor. Meanwhile, the supermarket floor has all its tiles and the tiles on the floor form an attractive flower design. A person tries to avoid the dirty neighborhood store but looks forward to entering the clean supermarket.

The neighborhood store clerks present a much more negative atmosphere than the supermarket store employees. In the corner grocery store, the workers insult the customers by calling them "idiots." Conversely, the employees at the supermarket smile and greet the customers with a warm "hello." In addition, although the cashiers at the neighborhood store throw the customers' change on the counter, the cashiers at the supermarket carefully place the money in the customers' hands. Furthermore, the employees at the neighborhood store talk on the phone and ignore the customers unlike the employees at the supermarket who ask how they can help the customer. A person feels abused at the neighborhood store and welcomed in the supermarket.

Given a choice between a supermarket and the neighborhood store, a smart person shops at the supermarket because she gets better prices, goes into a clean place, and gets more attention. A smart person will go without a product for a day or two until she can get to the supermarket.

To emphasize how this essay contrasts items, the students put a triangle around each contrast word. They read each contrast and put a *C+* (for a good contrast) or a *C?* (for a weak contrast). These pupils identify the pattern of "negative" item, contrast transition word, and "positive" item. You talk about how vivid the details are in each contrast.

After students have examined an exemplary contrast paragraph and a contrast essay, they fully comprehend what is really required of them. Through the use of exemplars, the learners go from a very conceptual understanding of a contrast essay to a very practical knowledge of what a contrast essay is. They are certain what a contrast essay is and what quality is required in such an essay. Furthermore, the writers know that these exemplars are available in a classroom binder, on the class website or the class wiki (an online collaborative website). The pupils are aware that they can find these exemplars online at anytime.

You may be asking, "But won't the students just copy the exemplar essay?" The students have to pick their own topics, develop their own categories, and create their own details. They develop their own ways of showing contrasts. The exemplar guides them and gives them support. Another way to think of the exemplar is as an Olympic diving event. Every swimmer does the same dive but adds his or her own style to it. Great artists do variations on other artists. Your students stand on the "shoulders of giants" so that their work becomes exemplary.

Immediately, you begin to collect exemplary work for the next time you teach each type of writing. When your students do an exemplary or almost exemplary piece of work, you put a preprinted mail label sticker on the top of their word processed paper that says "Great essay! Please email me a copy of this paper so that I may share it with future students. Thanks for helping them to be better writers. I may make some minor changes." If students hand in their papers electronically, you cut-and-paste the praise message ("Great essay. I might share it with future students. Thanks for helping them to be better writers.") on the top of their papers. You keep a copy of the students' rubric for any nearly exemplary writings to more easily make minor modifications to transform their writing into exemplary writing.

# 2

# Monitor Students' Writing

In the formative assessment monitoring stage, you observe and collect data on the specific writing goal in many diverse ways (Figure 2.1). The collection process can include the learners' perceptions about their writing, their performance on short activities, their peers' observations, your observations of their work, and their online activities. This monitoring involves collecting real-time data from the students based on where they are in the writing process at this moment. Data from a year ago or even from a month ago is outdated.

**Figure 2.1. Role of Monitoring in Formative Assessment**

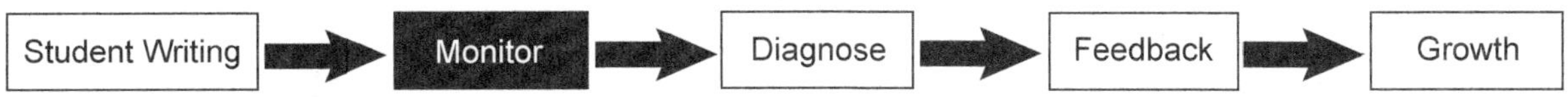


Formative assessment monitoring is embedded into the classroom. Collecting information at the beginning of the course is a great first collection tool. The students' baselines can be established and compared to additional information collected based on what they do during the class. However, most monitoring occurs within the daily writing in the classroom.

Once enough individual data is collected, usually a learning pattern emerges. The students are diagnosed based on the pattern.

This section contains:

- Previous Writing Types and Experiences
- Writing Sample
- Grammar Sample
- One-Minute Papers
- Write Alouds

## Previous Writing Types and Experiences

At the start of your English class, you do not know which types of writing your students have done previously and you do not know their writing strengths and weaknesses. Furthermore, you do not know what they think of as "good" writing. The more information you can find out about their writing before they start writing in your class, the better you can begin to develop appropriate feedback to help them to advance in their writing. You will also have information to redirect your instruction.

You might develop a short student self-perception survey that asks students to identify how many times they have done each specific type of writing, their strengths in each type of writing, and the areas for improvement for each type of writing (Figure 2.2). Ask them to complete the survey in a thoughtful manner so that you can better help them to improve. Your students can take this survey in paper format or in an online form through Blackboard, the free Google forms (http://docs.google.com), or the free part of Zoomerang (http://www.zoomerang.com). Once the students enter their responses, the online survey services will instantly calculate a class average for each numerical question and organize all of the responses for the same question together. You spend your time in analyzing the results instead of physically calculating the results and regrouping the information for each question.

**Figure 2.2. Writing Types Survey**

| **Name:** | | **Class:** | |
|---|---|---|---|
| Types of Previous Writing | Number of times you have done this writing | What are your major strengths in this type of writing? What do you do well in this type of writing? List 2 or 3. | What are your major areas for improvement in this type of writing? What do you need help in this type of writing? List 2 or 3. |
| Cause and Effect (Example: the three causes [reasons] for the Civil War or effects of it | | 1<br>2<br>3 | 1<br>2<br>3 |
| Argument or Persuasion (Example: convince someone to stop smoking) | | 1<br>2<br>3 | 1<br>2<br>3 |
| Classification (Example: the different types of cars, dogs, or friends) | | 1<br>2<br>3 | 1<br>2<br>3 |
| Compare and Contrast (Example: show the similarities or differences in pizza places) | | 1<br>2<br>3 | 1<br>2<br>3 |
| Research paper (Example: pick a topic, organize, research, get notes, and put paper together) | | 1<br>2<br>3 | 1<br>2<br>3 |

The calculated survey results reveal much information about your class's writing (Figure 2.3). In the following analysis, I calculated the percentage of the class that had completed each type of essay a certain number of times. Generally, the higher the number in the "0" and "1" columns such as "Compare and Contrast" and "Definition," the more you will develop in-depth explanations and exemplars when you present this writing to the class. You will begin to think of the students' usual learning gaps in these types of writing and prepare feedback materials.

**Figure 2.3. Previous Writing Analysis in Percent–Number of Times Having Done**

| Essay | 0 × | 1 × | 2 × | 3 × | 4 × | 5 × | 6 or more |
|---|---|---|---|---|---|---|---|
| Compare and Contrast | 10% | 20% | 20% | 20% | 10% | 10% | 10% |
| Argument/Persuasion | 10% | 10% | 0% | 10% | 20% | 20% | 30% |
| Definition Classification | 30% | 20% | 10% | 10% | 10% | 10% | 10% |
| Research Paper | 10% | 10% | 0% | 10% | 10% | 20% | 40% |

Likewise, their comments enable you to begin to understand their strengths and learning gaps. For instance, for "Compare and Contrast" writing, a student identifies her strengths as "(1) take time to collect many details; (2) can sort similarities and differences; and (3) like to get the opinions of others about my sort." She reveals her weaknesses as "(1) I need to know how to begin the paper; (2) I get confused in organizing the similarities and differences; and (3) I want to see some examples of this writing." After reading their comments, you get a strong feeling for what they think each type of writing is. You mentally compare their ideas with your expectations to help better your understanding of how to approach the particular type of writing.

You wonder what your students remember about what good writing is from their previous English experiences. Your students have had formal writing instruction since the early elementary grades. Which writing techniques do they remember? You can build on what they already know. Hopefully, you can learn some of the terms that they have used in the past that will connect their past learning to the new learning in this course. Based on their existing knowledge about writing, you can help them overcome learning gaps.

Ask your students to write down, individually, what they remember about "good" paragraph writing. This will be like the "K" in the KWL (Know, Want to Know, Learn) tool that some teachers use. Tell them that you want to know what they already know about paragraph writing so that you can move forward and not repeat things that they already know. They may think about a teacher saying, "You've done a great job. I especially like the way you...." Give the learners two to three minutes to list their ideas and have them draw a line under their last thought.

Next, have your students gather in small groups of three to six, and designate one student as the recorder. As each person contributes his or her list, the recorder (e.g., the student with the lightest colored shoes) creates a master list with no duplicates. One student reads the master list, and if the speaker lists a "good" writing idea that the other group members do not have, they write down that idea under the line they drew on their papers underneath their last individual thought.

When a group is done with the "good" ideas, the students look at their initial lists, the items above the line, and the additional items that their group suggested that are below the line. If they do not understand any writing technique that they have on their list, they ask their small group. They hand in to you the individual lists and the group lists. Then, you do the same process for essay writing.

After class analyze their lists. This quick activity provides some initial background information on the students. I did this activity with over forty students from two classes who formed six groups; the results are stated in terms of the percentage of the six groups that mentioned an item. If three groups had this item on their list, the score is 3/6 or 50% (Figure 2.4, left side).

All groups remembered grammar, punctuation, and spelling more than any other writing categories. They seemed focused on the mechanics of writing rather than on the content of writing. Only half of the groups identified details or main ideas as being important in writing an essay. Probably, their previous English teachers had the students go through the writing process for many years, but these students did not remember it.

Will the students' results on what makes a "good" essay reveal any different patterns than the paragraph results? I did this activity with thirty-four students who worked in five groups and generated the information on the right side of Figure 2.4.

Again, all groups identified spelling, grammar, and punctuation as being important. This time, indentation was a unanimous answer. Having a topic or thesis was also identified by all groups. Eighty percent identified the format of an essay such as introduction, conclusion, and paragraphs. Equally important to them was having a title and four paragraphs. Only two other answers, supporting details and references, were above 50%. Again the steps of the writing process were minimal. No group mentioned revision which is a critical part of the writing process.

These two collection tools, which each took about four minutes of class time and another five minutes each to analyze, give you much information about your class. Based on what the students expressed as the important parts of writing, you will help them to modify their thinking so that the expression of ideas becomes the most important part

**Figure 2.4. What Do Students Think of as "Good" Writing?**

| Paragraph "Good" Writing | Essay "Good" Writing |
|---|---|
| Proper grammar – 100%<br>Spelling – 100%<br>Correct punctuation – 100%<br>Details or facts – 50%<br>Main idea/topic - 50%<br>Inform the reader – 33%<br>Focused on one topic – 33%<br>Four to five sentences – 33%<br>Beginning, body & conclusion – 33%<br>Complete thoughts – 16%<br>No run on sentences -16%<br>Indented – 16%<br>Organized – 16%<br>Title – 16%<br>Research – 16%<br>Typed – 16%<br>Not too long (no more than 5 sentences) – 16% | Grammar – 100%<br>Spelling – 100%<br>Punctuation – 100%<br>Indentation - 100%<br>Topic/Thesis – 100%<br>Title – 80%<br>Paragraphs, at least four – 80%<br>Introduction – 80%<br>Conclusion – 80%<br>References/sources – 60%<br>Supporting details – 60%<br>Transition words – 40%<br>Quotes if needed – 40%<br>Body – 40%<br>Grab attention – 20%<br>Convince reader – 20%<br>Plagiarism – 20%<br>Brainstorm ideas – 20%<br>Formatting – 20%<br>Climax – 20% |

of writing, not the mechanics of writing such as punctuation. Likewise, since writing is a thinking process, you want them to be more aware of and to use the pre-writing phrase of the writing process.

## Writing Sample

What does the students' actual writing look like as they begin your class? Your school or you may have the students do a writing exercise during one of the first few classes of the year to measure the pupils' present writing skills

You may decide to give your students a writing exercise that is assessed with the state scoring rubric. Give a separate rating to each category of the rubric such as "Conventions -4" Next, create a spreadsheet with the students' names going down the column A starting at A2 (Figure 2.5). Label each of the writing categories going across row 2, starting at B2. Next, enter the students' individual scores going across their row, such as Brown's numbers starting at B3. By having the spreadsheet sum the column, you can see the class average. Likewise, you can program the spreadsheet to total the students' scores out of thirty (five columns each with the highest score being six is 5 × 6 or 30). Furthermore, you can sort each category by highlighting rows 2–6, selecting the sort function in your spreadsheet software, and sorting by the name of the category such as "Quality of Ideas" by ascending order (lowest to highest as in Figure 2.6) This information will quickly identify those with the lowest scores in that category so you can decide on small group or one-on-one instruction with these individuals.

**Figure 2.5. Writing Detailed Analysis**

| | A | B | C | D | E | F | G |
|---|---|---|---|---|---|---|---|
| 1 | ELA Writing Rubric | | | | | | |
| 2 | Student | Meaning | Development | Organization | Language Use | Convention | Total |
| 3 | Brown, Bob | 3 | 3 | 3 | 2 | 2 | 13 |
| 4 | Corin, BJ | 4 | 3 | 3 | 3 | 3 | 16 |
| 5 | Dunn, Ted | 5 | 4 | 4 | 4 | 4 | 21 |
| 6 | Evans, Ti | 2 | 2 | 2 | 2 | 2 | 10 |
| 7 | *Average* | 3.5 | 3 | 3 | 2.75 | 2.75 | 15 |

**Figure 2.6. Writing Sorted by Quality from Lowest to Highest**

| | A | B | C | D | E | F | G |
|---|---|---|---|---|---|---|---|
| 1 | ELA Writing Rubric | | | | | | |
| 2 | Student | Meaning | Development | Organization | Language Use | Convention | Total |
| 3 | Evans, Ti | 2 | 2 | 2 | 2 | 2 | 10 |
| 4 | Brown, Bob | 3 | 3 | 3 | 2 | 2 | 13 |
| 5 | Corin, BJ | 4 | 3 | 3 | 3 | 3 | 16 |
| 6 | Dunn, Ted | 5 | 4 | 4 | 4 | 4 | 21 |
| 7 | *Average* | 3.5 | 3 | 3 | 2.75 | 2.75 | 15 |

To get more detailed information now or at any time during the year, break the rubric categories into subparts or use a more detailed scoring tool. For example, you can focus on the category of development and specifically look for certain elements (Figure 2.7). You can score them on your state's scale or you can use a proficient scoring of 1 = nonproficient, 2 = developing, 3 = proficient, 4 = above proficient. You can program the spreadsheet to give averages for each element or totals for each student.

**Figure 2.7. Writing Development Scoring Tool**

| | A | B | C | D | E | F | G | H |
|---|---|---|---|---|---|---|---|---|
| 1 | ELA Writing Development | | | | | | | |
| 2 | | 5 Ps | Intro P | Thesis | Topic Sent | Evidence | Transitions | Conclud P |
| 3 | Evans, Ti | | | | | | | |
| 4 | Brown, Bob | | | | | | | |
| 5 | Corin, BJ | | | | | | | |
| 6 | Dunn, Ted | | | | | | | |

After all student have completed the writing activity, take about three-and-a-half minutes per individual to read over and record the information. Once you have finished entering the whole class' data, you now know the writing status of the class.

After doing this baseline writing assessment, you can prepare a quick class overview of the writing learning gaps that the vast majority of the class has. At the start of class, hand out their individual diagnoses based on the proficiency (1–4) scale (Figure 2.8). Then report back to the students the general class trends. Explain the specific learning problems, show the students a sentence or two with the problems, and provide one or more strategies to overcome them. Because they are aware of their learning gaps, they pay more attention to the improvement strategies.

**Figure 2.8. Writing Development Results to Be Given to a Student**

| | A | B | C | D | E | F | G | H |
|---|---|---|---|---|---|---|---|---|
| 1 | ELA Writing Development | | | | | | | |
| 2 | | 5 Ps | Intro P | Thesis | Topic Sent | Evidence | Transitions | Conclud P |
| 3 | Evans, Ti | 4 | 2 | 2 | 2 | 2 | 1 | 2 |

Because the writing collection tool reveals that certain groups of students share the same common learning gaps, in the future you will work with these small groups for more direct instruction. Then students will be listening to and participating in feedback activities that will directly assist them to overcome specific learning gaps. The instruction will be more differentiated for these young writers.

As you read students' future essays, you can jot down any other learning gaps so you can constantly be aware of their progress and the specific formative feedback that they need. You can check their future writing against these present learning gaps to see their improvement and to see areas in which they need focused assistance.

## Grammar Collection Tool

A grammar collection monitoring tool can discern students' specific strengths and learning gaps. As you use the writing collection tool, you can simultaneously use the grammar collection tool. Either use the state scoring rubric such as 1 (very low) to 6 (very high) or a proficiency rating of 1 (non proficient) to 4 (above proficient).

To be able to better analyze the grammar information, you can list the grammar topics and put them in a spreadsheet format (Figure 2.9). After the students have finished the writing activity, collect the papers. When you look at their writing for writing strengths and gaps, also look for specific grammar learning gaps. Record these in the same manner that you do the writing.

This quick monitoring reveals not only individual strengths and learning gaps, but also class strengths and gaps. For example, in one analysis you may discover that more than one quarter of the class has the grammar learning gap of improperly using an apostrophe for the plural of a word such as "man's." Such an analysis allows you to focus on overcoming the observed learning gaps.

As you read and assess the students' future writing, you can refer back to this grammar collection analysis. Students with deep grammar gaps show these gaps consistently, such as writing "cow's" for the plural of "cow." Occasionally you identify a student's grammar gap that did not show up in the first grammar collection tool. Again, look for a pattern of errors instead of a one-time only error.

**Figure 2.9. Teacher Grammar Collection Tool**

| | A | B | C | D |
|---|---|---|---|---|
| 1 | **Grammar Collection Tool** | | | |
| 2 | Name- initial only | Ed A. | Mar A. | Con B. |
| 3 | Nouns | | | |
| 4 | Determiners | | | |
| 5 | Prepositions | | | |
| 6 | Pronouns | | | |
| 7 | Adjectives and Adverbs | | | |
| 8 | Subject and Verbs | | | |
| 9 | Subject Verb Agreement | | | |
| 10 | Verb Tense Consistency | | | |
| 11 | Verb Past & Present Tense | | | |
| 12 | Verb Past Participles | | | |
| 13 | Verb Progressive Tense | | | |
| 14 | Verb Conditional, Gerund, Infinitives | | | |
| 15 | Sentence Fragment | | | |
| 16 | Sentence Run Ons | | | |
| 17 | Sentence Faculty Parallel Structure | | | |
| 18 | Sentence Combining | | | |
| 19 | Sentence Variety | | | |
| 20 | Exact Language | | | |
| 21 | Spelling | | | |
| 22 | Commonly Confused Words | | | |
| 23 | Commas, Periods | | | |
| 24 | Apostrophe | | | |
| 25 | Quotation Marks & Capitalization | | | |
| 26 | Contradictions | | | |
| 27 | Other: | | | |
| 28 | Other: | | | |

When students repeatedly show a grammar gap, move from the monitoring stage to the diagnosis stage. You can examine their learning gap to see how it differs from correct grammar and then determine which strategy will best assist the students. In the feedback stage, the learners receive brief written feedback which includes an explanation, a specific example of the grammar being used correctly, and an opportunity to practice this grammar. For example, for the grammar of using an apostrophe for the plural of a word, give the students the feedback shown in Figure 2.10.

**Figure 2.10. Apostrophe/Plurals Learning Gap**

To write a plural, usually add an "s"; do not use an apostrophe ('). For example, the plural of mother is mothers and the plural of toy is toys.

Dog's means the dog owns something like the dog's bone. The apostrophe (') shows possession, such as the man's car and the players' uniforms.

The plural of dog is dogs (more than one dog).

Write the plural of boy. ___________

Write that the boy owns something like a hat. The boy_ hat.

Write the plural of girl. __________

Write that a girl owns a purse The girl_ purse.

The textbook, on page 210, has some more practice exercises if you want to do them and then check the book's answer key.

You save these short grammar explanations in a word processor file called something like "Grammar Gaps." Because you are using a word processor, you can quickly copy this information the next time you observe the same grammar gap in another student. Instead of a word processing file, you can create a wiki (a collaborative online website; e.g., pbworks at http://pbworks.com) in which you put the grammar learning gaps and the many targeted activities for each gap so that students can access the information at anytime. If other teachers work with you to add to this wiki grammar gaps "bank," you all can develop an enormous bank of many diverse strategies for helping students to improve.

## One-Minute Papers

The previous monitoring involved creating a baseline of the students' strengths and learning gaps. The one-minute paper monitors what happens during the actual writing process.

A one-minute paper enables you to find out the learners' views of their strengths and learning gaps before they actually write their drafts. In the one-minute paper, the pupils look at the sentence starter and then complete each starter with a phrase, several phrases, or short sentences (Figure 2.11). As soon as they have completed the first sentence starter, they move to the next and continue until they have done a quick "brain dump" of their reflections about the writing. Students generally do take a little longer than a minute. However, keeping the time to less than three minutes prevents them from wandering; they focus more on the essentials in their quick reflections.

**Figure 2.11. One-Minute Writing Monitoring**

In this classification writing,

It is easy to _______ because _______.

I am doing well in _______ because _______.

I have had a little or some difficulty in _______. For example, _______.

I want to improve in _______.

Can I do this by myself or do I want help?

In class two days before the writers are to hand in their drafts, I have the students complete the one-minute paper about their essays. They can do this on paper or online in Blackboard, the free Google forms (http://docs.google.com) or the free part of Zoomerang (http://www.zoomerang.com). The learners are reminded that this one-minute paper is just a quick reflection on some key points about their papers, not a long documentary. After three minutes, all students have completed the form. If the pupils do this form online, then the results are available instantly; you can spend your time in analyzing the results rather than in collating them. Additionally, since they word process the form, their writing is legible.

Figures 2.12 and 2.13 are sample papers.

**Figure 2.12. Diana's One-Minute Paper**

Diana

In this argument writing,

It is easy to do everything really. There were handouts that gave great examples of how we were suppose to go about layering the paper.

I am doing well in keeping my ideas and details in the correct order, as well as developing a decent attention grabber and extension.

I have had a little or some difficulty in thinking of appropriate transitions other than the typical "furthermore" and "in addition."

I want to improve in being able to give more specific details.

Can I do this by myself or do I want help? I need help improving because how will I know what to work on if someone does not tell me what's wrong?

Diana's reflection identifies the strengths of her argument writing such as organized ideas, attention getter, and extension. Likewise, she states that some of her present writing gaps are using transitions and having specific details. Diana wisely realizes that she needs to know what is wrong before she can improve. This young student states she wants help. By comparing other students' papers to Diana's, you can identify whether her problems are the problems of the whole class, a small group of students, or just her own before you move on to diagnosis and feedback.

**Figure 2.13. Terry's One-Minute Paper**

Terry

In my classification writing,

It is easy to pick a topic and come up with 3 classifications for it.

I am doing well in giving good details in your classifications.

I have had a little or some problem in *coming up with a thesis.*

I want to improve in anything that isn't good.

Can I do this by myself or do I want help? I can do it by myself once I have some examples. I work better by myself.

Terry's reflection clearly demonstrates her writing strengths of picking a topic, having three classifications and giving details. Also, the reflection reveals her writing learning gap of coming up with a thesis. Her vague statement of "I want to improve on anything that isn't good" is not specific enough to help you to figure out what specific assistance she needs. If she cannot identify specific areas, then you will assist her in thinking of areas for improvement. Terry prefers to work by herself and she has identified that she only needs some examples. During class you can supply her with handouts or an online website to develop her skills.

As you read the students' reflections, record their writing strengths and gaps using a class listing. If they have done this online, their ideas are already organized. Some students in the class want help and others feels they can improve by themselves. There are small groups who have specific learning gaps; there are only a few learning gaps that are class wide. Classwide gaps can be covered during the next class periods.

After the students' drafts are peer reviewed or reviewed by you, go back and look at the students' one-minute comments to see how close their comments are to the diagnosis of their writing. Most students can honestly identify their learning gaps such as "using details." On the other hand, many students overestimate their success in the "It is easy to do" or "I do well in..." sections. This probably means they need more practice in comparing their views about the quality of writing to exemplars so that they can be sure of the high quality expected of them

## Write Alouds

As you read your students' essays, you wonder what they were thinking as they wrote their papers. Their prewrite showed organization, but then their minds seem to wander off in another direction or in multiple directions as they were actually writing their papers. You want to know more about what they are thinking as they write and how they view their own writing. By looking into their thinking through the use of a student write aloud, you can figure out the learning gaps between their starting organization and their final writing. Hopefully, the write aloud will allow you to view the hidden ideas like the eight-ninths of an iceberg that is below the water's surface. Instead of having the students do a verbal think aloud, you will ask them to write down their ideas in a writing think aloud.

Because the students will do the think aloud while they are writing, they need a form to guide their write aloud (Figure 2.14). In class they look at the write aloud form and listen as you give a short example of a think aloud as you write about the persuasive topic of "passing the course." For example, you say, "This essay is a persuasive essay so I have to convince or persuade my readers. I have done some of these in the past so I somewhat know what I have to do. I can convince my readers of what they need to do to pass this course. Maybe I can argue that to pass the course, students should have perfect attendance. That sounds like an interesting thesis. I think I can prove it. I need some proof. Let me think of anything that might prove it. What are the advantages of being in class all the time? I'll list my ideas as I say them. When students are in class, they hear the teacher explain the information. They can ask questions about how to do the homework. That's two reasons, I want to think more. What's another benefit of being in class each day?" After this modeling, students are ready to write down their thinking as they are doing the writing, not afterwards.

Next, the learners read the topic sentence, "The school should eliminate all finals," and develop a paragraph as they practice a mini-write aloud. They work on the writing passage for about a minute and then start their write aloud. Then they go back to writing and then back to the write aloud. As a class, you review these to make sure that the students' internal thinking is showing through and not their "what should I say to get a good grade" thinking.

As they do their next writing, have your students complete a full write aloud form. This thinking aloud form has large spaces between each category so that the pupils can write as much as they want without feeling like they are running out of space.

### Figure 2.14. Write Aloud Form

**Write Aloud**

As you think through and do the writing assignment, jot down your thoughts:

Doing this type of writing:

Selecting a topic:

Creating a topical sentence/thesis:

Doing the Prewrite: What type do you use? Does it help you generate many ideas about the topic? Does it help you organize your writing?

Adding transitions and vivid words to your prewrite to better organize your writing before you write:

Doing the first draft: Can you easily develop your writing from your prewrite?

Reading through and revising:

Checking your writing against the checklist:

Revising the essay after doing the checklist:

Your feeling about your writing after revising it:

Figure 2.15 is a sample of Kelly's write aloud for illustration writing.

### Figure 2.15. Kelly's Write Aloud

Doing this type of writing:

*If I read the handout again, I can better understand the format and how the essay is supposed to be written. I read the sample writing since it shows me how to do it and I look at the format.*

Selecting a topic:

*This was the hardest part of the essay. I look at the writing topics and think that I could write about several of them. Which one will I use? I think about each one. After a long time, I pick one.*

Creating a topical sentence/thesis:

*Thinking of a good topic sentence was challenging. I know the topic sentence should give the purpose of the whole paragraph but I just want to start writing about the topic.*

Doing the Prewrite: What type did you use? Did it help you generate many ideas about the topic? Did it help you organize your writing?

*I did a brainstorm listing and then used a graphic organizer. After brainstorming, I did not have much trouble in completing the graphic organizer. It is an effective way to organize my ideas.*

Adding transitions and vivid words to your prewrite to better organize your writing before you write:

*I add transitions as I do the draft, not in the prewrite graphic organizer. Sometimes I forget to put them in. I have trouble in thinking of vivid words, I use the usual transition words.*

Doing the first draft: Can you easily develop your writing from your prewrite?

*I find it very useful to use this method of prewriting. I put each part of the prewrite into its own paragraph.*

Reading through and revising:

*I felt that doing a prewrite minimized revising. I used the spell check since I'm not a good speller. I added some more details after reading it through.*

Checking your writing against the checklist:

*It is helpful to make sure I have not forgotten anything.*

Revising the essay after doing the checklist:

*Easier because I know what I am missing. Since I do it on the computer, it's not as bad to make changes.*

Your feeling about your writing after revising it:

*Exhausted. I think I did a good job.*

Kelly's write aloud reveals her self-perceived writing strengths and areas where she feels she needs help. You can have a one-on-one with her to help her overcome her learning gap of topic sentences as she always has a strong thesis. She will be put in a small group for direct instruction in transitions along with others with the same learning gap.

# 3

# Diagnose Students' Writing

Now that you understand the writing standards and have collected some real-time information through monitoring the students' writing, you begin to diagnose their strengths and their areas for improvement (Figure 3.1). In the first part of the diagnosis process, you compare the present status of the students to the expected level in the standard. You identify the students' specific learning strength(s) or learning gap(s) by name. A critical problem in formative assessment is that the teachers do not identify the exact learning strength or gap by a name, so they cannot see if the student has already mastered the skill or still has to overcome the gap. For example, after you compare Vadra's contrast essay to the exemplar, you identify that her essay lacks sequencing, specifically she lacks contrast transition words.

**Figure 3.1. The Role of Diagnosis in Formative Assessment**

In the second part of the diagnosis process, you select an appropriate strategy that will move the students forward in their writing to the expected level if they have not already reached it. Because Vadra does not use contrast transition words, you can ask her to do a series of exercises that enable her to identify the meaning of the transitions, see how these transitions are used, and write sentences with contrast transition words. For instance, one exercise has two opposite ideas such as "The first worker earns eight dollars an hour, _______ the second worker earns twelve dollars an hour " and Vadra inserts a contrast transition word from the provided list.

Often the process of going from monitoring to diagnosing happens in a split second. The observation of a student immediately leads to the diagnosis. At other times, the collected data has to be sifted through before any diagnosis can be done. Likewise, the process of diagnosis can be a split-second decision; the student's learning gap is _____ and the student can do _____ to improve. At other times, the diagnosis process involves a lengthy process to identify the precise learning gap or to select a truly effective strategy for a particular student.

## Scaffolding

If students write " I don't know what to do", "I'm confused. Help!", "I need some organization", and "I wander and then get lost" in their one minute papers and mini-think alouds, they are demonstrating the learning gap of underdeveloping an essay. As you read their statements and look at their present lack of process in writing, you diagnose them as needing a scaffold (Figure 3.2). Some writers need a step-by-step or hand-holding approach to guide them through the writing process for an essay. Therefore you create scaffolded material that can provide individual assistance through its high structure. Figure 3.3 is an example of a partial scaffold for classification writing. Start this scaffolding with a definition of the type of writing (such as classification), give some real life examples of classification, explain the structure for classification writing, supply an exemplar, provide an "I can" list of the steps in writing a classification essay, and supply some classification topics, a large blank graphic organizer, and a final checklist (Figure 3.3). The learners can follow the hand-holding materials to guide them through the process.

**Figure 3.2 Scaffolded Bridges**

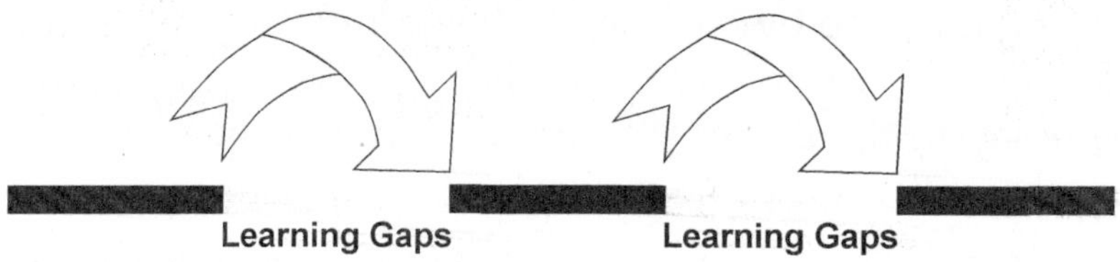


**Figure 3.3. Partial Scaffold for Classification Writing**

**Classification Writing**

Classification is a type of definition writing.

When you classify, you *sort a topic into understandable categories. Each category is very different from the other.* You classify products, TV shows, teachers, and events. You might categorize events into social, sports, and music

*Real-life uses:*

Stores classify the types of products like ice cream.

Car dealerships classify types of vehicles such as trucks.

Gardeners classify the types of flowers such as roses.

Insurance companies categorize drivers as younger than age 18.

You classify homework as to when it is due: tomorrow, this week, in a month.

*Classification chart: Types of*

Topic:

| 1st Category: | 2nd Category: | 3rd Category: |
|---|---|---|
| Characteristics: | Characteristics: | Characteristics: |
| A | A | A |
| B | B | B |
| C | C | C |
| D | D | D |

*Some writing topics: Types of … or you can add any topic you know much about*

| | | | |
|---|---|---|---|
| Internet sites | Buildings | Friends/Parents | Clothing |
| Bosses/Teachers/ Students | Organizations | Music | Restaurants |
| Courses/Classes | Sports/Exercise/ Hobbies | Animals/Pets | Stores |
| TV shows/movies/video games | | Cars/Trucks/Boats/Trains/Planes/Bikes/ Skates | |

I can *(partial)*

- ___ Select or create a topic that has many classifications.
- ___ Identify three different classifications within that topic.
- ___ Make sure that the three classifications are very different and do not overlap.
- ___ Define each classification.
- ___ Supply a concrete example that illustrates each classification.
- ___ Decide on the order of the three classifications.
- ___ Brainstorm four common characteristics for these classifications.
- ___ Make sure that the common characteristics are very different and do not overlap.
- ___ Arrange the characteristics in a logical sequence or order.

When these struggling students turn in their classification essays, they reflect, "The essay was easy; all I had to do was follow the handout," or "When I was unsure of what to do, I checked the handout," and "The handout keep me from getting off track." You know that you have provided them with the high structure that they need. When you assess their essays and find them to be of a high quality, you are confident that this diagnosis did move the students forward in their writing.

# 4

# Formative Feedback For Students

Once you have collected information about the students (monitored), diagnosed their present position in regard to the learning goal, and diagnosed an appropriate strategy that will directly move them forward, you are ready to give the students formative feedback (Figure 4.1) to help them improve in their writing.

**Figure 4.1. The Role of Feedback in Formative Assessment**

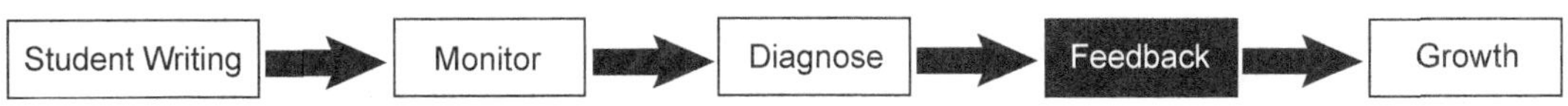


Formative feedback focuses on how and what is said to the students so that they will (1) understand what you said, (2) emotionally accept what is being said, (3) be willing to make a change, and (4) actually implement the change. Bender (2007) stresses that an encouraging coaching attitude is a critical factor in giving feedback.

**Figure 4.2 Formative Feedback to Change**

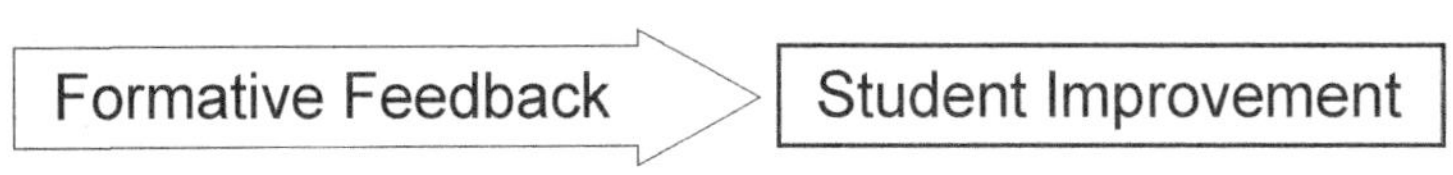


Students respond best to feedback when the feedback comments are based directly on their own work. They do not want to hear general feedback statements such "many of you" or "some of you." However, depending on the number of learners who have the same learning gap, you may give whole class, small group, or individual feedback.

This sections contains:

- ♦ General Feedback Suggestions
- ♦ Peer Feedback Improvements
- ♦ Objective Peer Feedback

# General Feedback Suggestions

## Limit the Feedback

"Red pen depression" syndrome occurs when students see so many comments on their papers, they are overwhelmed. They feel that they have so many changes to make that they cannot even start to make any changes. Depressed people feel that there is nothing they can do to change their world; likewise, students whose papers are covered with negative comments feel that their writing world is hopeless.

Formative assessment stresses that you select those very few, two or three, specific areas that are the most critical to a student's writing success, and then you give comments in only those areas. For example, an area for improvement may be "using topic sentences." Because students have only two to three areas to improve in, they feel that they can make changes in these few areas. When students make these critical changes, their writing drastically improves from their previous writing.

Because you are focusing on only two to three critical areas, you can include very specific feedback that indicates precisely how the students are to change and examples to guide the students to success. You have more time to write important comments that will lead directly to students' success as you are not commenting on every error the students make. With precise feedback, students can better overcome these critical learning gaps.

For example, you can identify three areas for improvement by either listing them at the bottom of the students' writing or by numbering them in the actual writing. Clearly identify the learning gap, give an example, and provide a strategy for improvement. Take time in writing these as these are the three areas that you expect the student to improve in from this essay to the next. Comments for your student, Ty, are as follows:

1. *Clearly state the thesis.* A thesis states the purpose of the writing. "Hybrid cars are great" does not tell the reader what the purpose of the paper is; however, "All Americans should buy hybrid cars" clearly defines the purpose of the paper. A thesis has a topic and strong position on that topic; "All Americans" is the topic and the strong position is "should buy hybrid cars." You can change your sentence to be a thesis statement by including the topic and the strong position.
2. *Use a topic sentence.* Start your paragraph with a restatement of the thesis and then the specific category that will prove it. For example, in the topic sentence of "Using hybrid cars results in less dependence on foreign oil," "Using hybrid cars" is the thesis restatement and "results in less dependence on foreign oil" is the controlling idea or category of proof for the paragraph. Look at your thesis and the category of proof, then rewrite your topic sentence.
3. *Use contrast transition words.* You can show differences between two sentences by using a contrast word such as "however" or "conversely." For example, you can add a contrast word to the sentences "A Hyundai Sonata

gets twenty-three miles to a gallon. A Toyota Prius gets thirty-nine miles to a gallon." to emphasize the difference: "A Hyundai Sonata gets twenty-three miles to a gallon. However, a Toyota Prius gets thirty-nine miles to a gallon." Look at your transition word handout and put a contrast transition word between the differences.

Be precise; avoid vague feedback.

Many learners do not make changes to their essays when comments are vague or meaningless to them. When students read the comments such as "Try harder," "Focus," "Organize your ideas," "Rewrite," and "Do better," they have no idea how to change. Likewise, they may read the following editing codes (Figure 4.3) on their papers (Figure 4.4).

**Figure 4.3. Vague Editing Codes**

Ag = agreement subject/verb *or* pronoun/antecedent

Awk = awkward

Frag = fragment

NP = new paragraph

P/A = pronoun/antecedent agreement

Pron = pronoun

R-O - run-on

SP = spelling

S/V = subject/verb agreement

Tr = transition

Voc = vocabulary

**Figure 4.4. Vague Editing Codes Used in Student Writing**

| If a teenager has a dream of going to college and wants to have a bright future, it is a dream that will do them well. Lastly, when an adult has a dream house that they want when they retire, it makes them feel safe. If a person comes along and destroys that dream, the adult's mind is messed up and will have to start all over thinking where and when to get a new house. | Awk<br>Pron<br>Voc |
|---|---|

The students see the first comment of "Awk" but they are not sure which part of which sentence the comment "Awk" is describing. Although the learning gap is identified, the gap comment does not match up directly with a specific word, phrase, or sentence. Even if the students know that "Awk" means "awkward," they do not know what specifically is awkward. Even if the teacher circles "do them well," the student still does not know what is "awkward" about this statement. Lastly, the student probably does not know how to improve the sentence, which is the second part of the diagnosis. If they really understood "Awk," then most likely they would not have written the sentence in this way. Thus a comment that seems like a wonderful diagnostic help such as "Awk" really is ineffective.

You can change from vague to specific comments by focusing on critical skills. Identify the learning gap (subject/verb agreement), tell how to correct it (check to make sure a singular noun has a singular pronoun) and give an example (gap: "The *boy* found *their* pen." "Boy" is singular but "their" is plural so change the sentence to "The boy found his pen" or "The boys found their pens"). When students read such precise feedback, they know precisely how to improve.

## Feedback Format

If students who are struggling writers hear negative comments about their writing, they will not feel like changing. Likewise, fairly good writers may not be receptive to suggestions for changes. How can students feel that they are being invited, not demanded, to make changes? How can they feel like they are in control of their writing and not simply controlled by the teacher?

Oral or written feedback can be given in such a way that the students feel that feedback is targeted for them and that feedback will directly assist them in becoming better writers. One oral feedback model (Figure 4.5) is a variation on Brookhart's (2008) model.

**Figure 4.5. Oral Feedback Model**

1. Student name.
2. Mention that you have been reading the student's writing.
3. Identify something the student has done well in the writing and give an example of it. *Pause*
4. State that you have noticed another pattern in the student's writing and tell what it is. *Pause*
5. Identify the learning gap by name and explain why it is a learning gap.
6. Mention that there is a way that other students have used to improve in this area. Name the strategy and give an example of it. *Pause*
7. Invite the student to try this new strategy.

For example, this formative feedback for lack of topic sentences might look like this: "Juan, I have been looking at your writing and I've noticed that you do a great job in writing your thesis. You clearly state the purpose of your paper (*pause*). Also, I've noticed that some of your topic sentences do not tell the purpose of the paragraph (*pause*). Many successful writers use a technique called restating to write better topic sentences. Would you like to try it?"

One approach to formative feedback is the "sandwich approach" in which students hear good news about their learning, then the bad news, and possibly more good news about their learning. Students need to hear at least three positive comments before they believe the comments are really positive. Any less than three and they translate the comments as negatives; therefore, they begin to feel the "red pen syndrome" of their inability to improve.

Another method of giving oral feedback occurs after students have reflected on their drafts. You ask them some questions to help them think through their work such as: "What do you feel were your strengths in this writing?" "What areas do you think could be improved?" "What other strategies might you use?" These and additional questions can help them figure out new solutions to their learning gaps.

## Peer Feedback Improvements

Students can help each other to improve in a formative assessment approach. Figure 4.6 illustrates the stages of peer review. However, according to students, what happens during peer review does not often help them improve their writing.

**Figure 4.6 Peer Review Stages**

Pre-Peer Review ⟶ Peer Review ⟶ Post-Peer Review

Before students have their writing peer reviewed, they can give the reviewer an overview of their work. Several students comment that the review would be more meaningful "if the person really understood what I was trying to say." If the reviewer clearly understands the intended purpose of the paper, the reviewer can do a better job of reviewing the work. The reviewer can make sure that the author achieves his or her purpose in the writing. Students may take from thirty seconds for a short paper (one to two pages) to a minute for a long paper (three plus pages) to give an oral overview of their work. The author's overview only touches on the purpose and major points of the report; it does not explain all the details.

If students are going to do many peer reviews on the same project, they can partner with the same person throughout the peer review. If the learners are going to peer review other learners' thesis statements, graphic organizers, topic sentences, paragraphs, and their draft essays, then they would prefer to do it with the same person. Once the reviewer understands the thesis, he or she spends less time figuring out the paper's purpose; the reviewer focuses more on the writer's strengths and gaps. With the same reviewer throughout the process, the reviewer can see changes in the author's paper that a new reviewer for each part of the paper probably would not notice.

The students want the reviewer to conduct an objective evaluation of the paper. They do not want to know what the reviewer "feels" about their writing with statements such as "I really like your motorcycle section. I've always wanted one." As one student states, "I don't care if he likes my paper or not; I care how well I did." Students stress that the real reason for the review is to have the reviewer identify their successes and problems. Likewise, the reviewers have to thoroughly understand the assessment tool before they can assess another student's work. These reviewers can use the class rubric or checklist of "I can" statements as the "yardstick" against which to measure the author's paper.

The authors want the reviewer to move from just identifying a problem to telling them how to improve it. A student complains, "The reviewer sees a problem but does not tell me how to fix it. Why bother?" and another writes, "There are never suggestions, only things I am missing." Students are willing to correct their problems once they know how. Sometimes a peer reviewer's identification of the problem also includes the solution such as "You are missing the topic sentence; put it in." At other times, the peer reviewer has to figure out the problem and suggest how to remedy the problem with a statement like, "Your classification characteristics in each body paragraph are not in the same order. You might use the order in each body paragraph (1) mower size, (2) lawn size, (3) mower speed, and (4) mower cost."

In a similar vein, after the writers read over the peer comments and think about the possible improvements, they have the reviewer orally explain the comments for improvement. Even though the reviewer has written several comments, often times an author reads a comment and is unsure of what the comment means. One student indicates that she would make more improvements "if it was easier to understand what the reviewer was saying." The writers want the reviewer to verbally go over each major comment and explain how to make it better.

## Objective Peer Feedback

As students go through the writing process, you want them to be able to peer review. However, do they understand what a "peer review" really entails? When most students are asked what they think they will do when they look over another student's paper, they write that they will correct their grammar, spelling, and punctuation. They do not realize the critical difference between proofing for mechanical errors and revising for clarity. Their focus should be on revision, or helping the other student to improve the ideas in the paper. Once there are good ideas in the paper, it can be edited or proofread for grammar, spelling, and punctuation.

Also, you want to use a technique that is neither confrontational nor seems like a negative critique of anyone. Most students comment that writing feedback has been a very negative experience. In the past, their writing has been so "covered in red" that they cannot even see their original writing. They dread getting back their reviewed papers.

Stress that the reviewer is trying to help the writers better express their ideas. If the reviewer does not understand an idea, then the authors have probably not communicated it very well. Writers should not get upset with the reviewer as the reviewer's sole purpose is to help the writers improve. Share with them the saying, "Do not shoot the messenger."

In addition, you want to use a technique that gives the students definite formative feedback about their writing. They will be able to see their strengths and learning gaps through this quick peer evaluation. They will know what to do to improve. Likewise, the evaluator will become more aware of the critical components of expressing ideas.

After students have written their drafts, they exchange their essays. Students spend thirty seconds to a minute explaining their papers to the reviewer. Then they use a peer evaluation form (Figure 4.7) to help them "mark up" another student's paper. After about ten minutes, they return the papers to the owners (Figure 4.9, page 45, is an example of an unmarked essay and Figure 4.10, page 46, illustrates the same essay marked up). These writers can tell by looking at all the marks what their strengths are. When students do not have many marks, they can look at the peer-evaluation form and find out their specific learning gaps. After they have looked over their papers, they confer with the peer reviewer to get more clarification about how they can improve.

**Figure 4.7. Peer Markup: Shapes**

- Put a large exclamation (*!*) next to the attention getter in the introduction if it interests you in the topic.
- Put a *box* around the thesis if it states the topic and a controlling idea.
- Put a *box* around each topic sentence if it includes the thesis topic and controlling idea of proof for the paragraph.
- Put a *box* around the first sentence in the concluding paragraph if it restates the thesis.
- In each body paragraph, *circle* each piece of evidence.
- In each body paragraph, *underline* each specific detail that supports the evidence.
- Put a *triangle* around the transition words.
- Put a large *E* next to the extender in the conclusion if it extends the idea past the thesis.
- At the bottom of the bottom:
  - Write two or more positives about this paper.
  - What area would you like the author to clarify for you?

Some students prefer a color coding in which the thesis, topic sentence, and thesis restatement are in red highlighter, the evidence has a yellow color, the details have a green color, and the sequencing words such as transitions are purple (you can use a yellow highlighter over a red highlighter to make purple).

In another version (Figure 4.8) of markups, students indicate the presence or absence of various elements.

**Figure 4.8. Student Markup: Letters**

In the introductory paragraph, if the attention getter draws you into the writing, write *A+* next to it. If not, write *A?*.

In the introductory paragraph, if the thesis is clearly stated write *TH+*. If not, write *TH?*.

In each body paragraph, if the topic sentence paraphrases the thesis and then tells the category (purpose of the paragraph), then write *T+*. If not, write *T?*.

In each body paragraph, if there is specific evidence, write *E+*. If not, write *E?*. At the end of each paragraph, indicate how many *E+*s there are by writing *E+ = (the number)* such as *E+ = 3*.

In each body paragraph, if there is a specific detail for the pieces of evidence, then write *S+* above each detail. If the detail, is not specific, then write *S?*. At the end of each paragraph, indicate how many *S+*s there are such as *S+ = 6*.

The first time your class does a "markup" peer review, one student, Sam, remarks that he does not want anyone to write on his paper. However, when he receives his paper back with many positive marks on it, a smile appears on his face. He looks forward to seeing positive marks. The students do not receive negative comments but positive marks or no comments. Students like that they receive instant feedback on their writing. With this method of peer review, students look forward to having many marks on their papers because each mark indicates that they have included essential components of writing.

Students have an almost instant reaction to the peer-review box, underlines and circles. As one student shared with his peer reviewer upon receiving his paper back, "I need more evidence since I don't see any circles." Another student commented to her peer reviewer, "Look at how much better I'm doing! All of my topic sentences are in boxes." Although this feedback does not provide concrete suggestions for improvements, the students are aware of their learning gaps. They know that in-class and online resources will help them overcome these gaps.

A further benefit to doing the in class peer evaluation is that the students get immediate feedback. In many English courses, students often do not get their draft papers back for a week or more. Formative feedback stresses that the sooner the students get feedback, the more meaningful it is to them and the more likely the learners are to act on the feedback.

An unanticipated advantage of the in-class peer evaluation is that you can evaluate draft papers more quickly once you see all the peer evaluation "markups." A peer has already identified the strengths. You can double check the essay and then score the essay rubric along with a few specific suggestions for improvements.

## Figure 4.9. Classification Essay Without Any Markups

People do more than get hungry, they get hungry for their favorite restaurant food. What type of restaurants do people prefer for their favorite food? Restaurants can be divided into fast food, sit down, and fancy.

Fast food restaurants like McDonald's are good for "on the go" food. McDonald's charges about six dollars for a combo meal that consists of a hamburger, French fries, and a drink. Similarly, the food variety is slim with options being mostly variations on hamburgers and the size of the fries. Likewise, the atmosphere at McDonald's is very cafeteria-like with bright colors and lights. Furthermore, there is no waitress so people have to take the food to a table on a tray and then throw out the garbage before they leave.

When there is a little more time to spare, a good choice for eating out is a sit down restaurant like Applebee's. The cost for food at Applebee's ranges from ten to twenty dollars for a meal. In addition, the food selection is extensive, offering tasty meals like steak, pasta, chicken, and fancy salads. Moreover, the atmosphere at Applebee's is more relaxing. People can look at pictures on the wall or watch televisions to keep themselves entertained while waiting for their food. With the decoration and televisions, they have many topics for conversation. Also, a waitress serves the customers.

For special eating out occasions, there are fancier restaurants like Lascas. A meal starts at the price of twenty dollars at this luxury restaurant. Specifically, the food choices at Lascas are more sophisticated with lobster and fillet minion. Next, the ambiance at Lascas is more intimate with low lighting, quiet surroundings, and neutral colors. The customers focus on their dining companion rather than the restaurant. In addition, the restaurant uses linen tablecloths and cloth napkins. Fancy restaurants usually have a waitress, a water/coffer server, and even a wine server to make the eating experience more enjoyable.

A person can select a fast food, a sit down or a fancy restaurant based on price, food and atmosphere to fit their dining desire. No matter which restaurant, there are no pots and pans to clean!

## Figure 4.10. Marked Up Essay

People do more than get hungry, they get hungry for their favorite restaurant food. What type of restaurants do people prefer for their favorite food? Restaurants can be divided into fast food, sit down, and fancy.

Fast food restaurants like McDonald's are good for "on the go" food. McDonald's charges about six dollars for a combo meal that consists of a hamburger, French fries, and a drink. Similarly, the food variety is slim with options being mostly variations on hamburgers and the size of the fries. Likewise, the atmosphere at McDonald's is very cafeteria-like with bright colors and lights. Furthermore, there is no waitress so people have to take the food to a table on a tray and then throw out the garbage before they leave.

When there is a little more time to spare, a good choice for eating out is a sit down restaurant like Applebee's. The cost for food at Applebee's ranges from ten to twenty dollars for a meal. In addition, the food selection is extensive, offering tasty meals like steak, pasta, chicken, and fancy salads. Moreover, the atmosphere at Applebee's is more relaxing. People can look at pictures on the wall or watch televisions to keep themselves entertained while waiting for their food. With the decoration and televisions, they have many topics for conversation. Also, a waitress serves the customers.

For special eating out occasions, there are fancier restaurants like Lascas. A meal starts at the price of twenty dollars at this luxury restaurant. Specifically, the food choices at Lascas are more sophisticated with lobster and fillet minion. Next, the ambiance at Lascas is more intimate with low lighting, quiet surroundings, and neutral colors. The customers focus on their dining companion rather than the restaurant. In addition, the restaurant uses linen tablecloths and cloth napkins. Fancy restaurants usually have a waitress, a water/coffer server, and even a wine server to make the eating experience more enjoyable.

A person can select a fast food, a sit down or a fancy restaurant based on price, food and atmosphere to fit their dining desire. No matter which restaurant, there are no pots and pans to clean!

## Online Writing Assessments

Unfortunately, there is only one of you in the classroom. You want to give each of your twenty-five or more students immediate feedback on their writing, but immediate feedback to that many students becomes extremely difficult. Online programs can give instant online feedback to students (Figure 4.11). Students submit their writing electronically and within seconds or minutes, they have instant feedback on their writing. This immediate feedback provides a good starting point for students to help them identify their strengths and gaps.

**Figure 4.11 Online Paper Assessment**

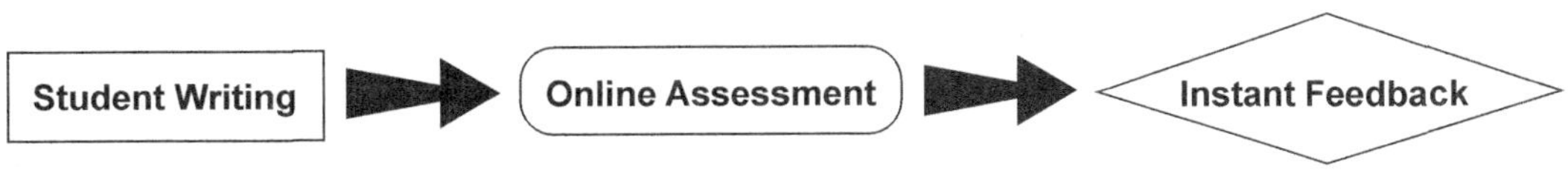


MY Access! (http://www.vantagelearning.com/school/products/myaccess/features.html), " is an online instructional program for students in grades 4–12 and at the college level that is designed to increase student literacy. When students write essays using MY Access!, the program assesses their writing ability and provides developmentally appropriate suggestions for improvement. By grading student essays within seconds of submission and providing detailed feedback, MY Access! enriches the education experience, giving teachers more time to teach writing instruction to their classes and monitor student progress over time."

This program gives a holistic score to the student's writing and then gives individual scores for focus and meaning, content and development, organization, language use, voice, and style (Figure 4.12).

**Figure 4.12. MY Access! Chart (Score out of 6)**

| Holistic Score 2.4 | Content & Development 2.1 | Organization 2.1 |
|---|---|---|
| Focus & Meaning 2.2 | Mechanics & Conventions 2.2 | Language Use, Voice & Style 2.5 |

MY Access! allows the students to develop a revision plan by answering guided comments such as "Does my introductory paragraph start with an attention grabber (a quotation, startling fact, dialogue, or a story)?" It allows them to see exemplar writing done in the type of writing they are doing so they can compare their writing to the exemplar. In addition, students can access the MyTutor function to receive instructional feedback prior to or after submitting their essay for a score. This feedback is broken down by domain/trait and provides a variety of instructional suggestions to improve the essay.

In Pearson's Intelligent Essay Assessor (http://www.pearsonkt.com/prodIEA.shtml), students from elementary through college submit their writing and the program assesses it. The program reports the score out of 6 and provides comments in four major categories (as taken from the website in Figure 4.13).

**Figure 4.13. Pearson's Intelligent Essay Assessor Chart**

| Audience and Purpose | Organization | Elaboration | Use of Language |
|---|---|---|---|
| While the prompt may be addressed, the main idea may not be clear | May have organization in parts, but lacks organization in other parts | The support given for the thesis may be unclear or undeveloped | Inconsistent control of sentence structure, and incorrect word choices; errors in spelling, grammar, or punctuation occasionally interfere with reader understanding |

The program also lists the students' spelling and grammatical errors.

Smartthinking.com (http://www.smarthinking.com/) serves public schools as well as colleges. This program provides tutors through live chats. The tutor clarifies the writing assignment with the student and either helps the student get started or reacts to the student's work. The tutor constantly asks questions of the student to guide the student through the writing process. Figure 4.14 is an example of a student's writing with the Smartthinking comments in italics.

**Figure 4.14. Smarthinking Feedback**

> Preparation differs for a trip by bus and one by car. In a bus, one's luggage is loaded from outside the box into a compartment under the bus. There is no access to it until the person's destination is reached. Plan your carry-on with care, as its contents need to meet the person's entire trip's requirement. *(This is advice, and that isn't the purpose of the paper. How can you describe your own preparation for a bus trip?)* On the other hand, when a person packs the car, the luggage is easily accessible and the front seat can be the location for the tote bag contents. *(If you think that driving a car is more convenient, then emphasize it more to show the difference.)*

In Smartthinking, students can access the "Drop-in" for live tutoring, submit questions for a response within 24 hours, preschedule sessions, and view archives of past sessions.

There are many advantages to these programs. First, students get feedback within seconds. In many cases, they receive a "rating" on the various aspects of writing. Also, the online tutor can give personal help to the student. However, there are also drawbacks. These programs sometimes give general feedback. When the students receive back statements such as "lacks organization in some parts," they do not know where they lack organization. These struggling writers do not have any feedback that is targeted to their specific gap as it appears in their paper. You may have students use online assessment as an advanced form of peer review where they receive instant feedback and some suggestions for change.

# 5

# Time For Students' Growth

When your writers have been monitored, diagnosed for their learning strength or gap, offered a strategy, and given feedback in a friendly and inviting manner, they are ready to overcome their learning gap (Figure 5.1). When young writers are given time immediately after receiving formative feedback to practice and improve, they make tremendous gains (Figure 5.2). The more they delay their practice and potential improvement, the less likely they are to succeed. Medicine has the "golden hour" concept of immediacy; the greatest chance for survival of a person with multisystem trauma is within the first sixty minutes after the trauma. Our students' golden "hour" is the time immediately after receiving the feedback; their "golden hour" is about fifteen minutes. Once they leave the classroom their likelihood of improving decreases dramatically. Also, criminal detectives report that the chance of solving a crime decreases drastically with time. The chance of students overcoming a learning gap also decreases drastically with time.

**Figure 5.1. The Role of Growth in Formative Assessment**

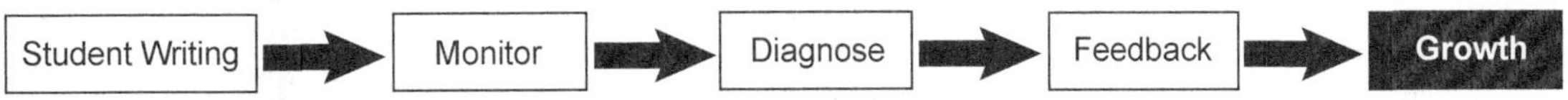


**Figure 5.2. Time for Growth**

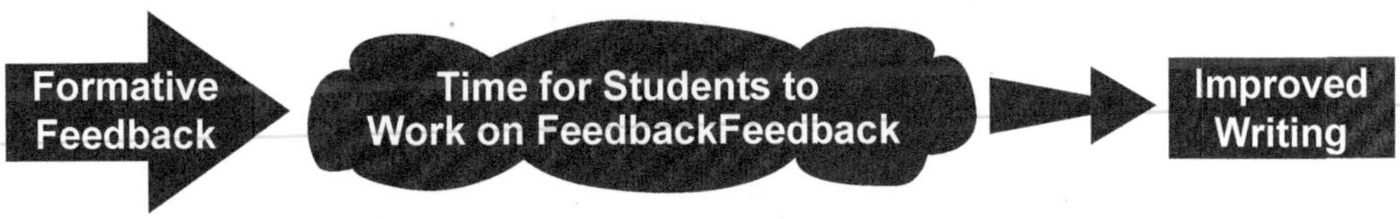


After you have assessed your students' writing, you will want to spend whole-class time in going over the learning gaps that the whole class displayed. In order to focus on helping as many students as possible at a time, go from whole-class feedback and time for improvement, to small-group feedback and time for improvement, and then individual feedback and time for improvement. For example, if more than ninety percent of the class showed the learning gap of "paragraph development," then you give the whole-class feedback and time for growth on "paragraph development." Then you move down to the next greatest number of students who have the same learning gap.

If fifty percent of the class has the learning gap of "details," you can meet with half the class.

You will want to build in class time after each formative feedback for students to grow. Depending on the number of learners who have the same learning gap you probably will have several small groups, each with different learning gaps (Figure 5.3). Small groups provide differentiation for your students. The secret to these small groups' success is very targeted materials that will lead directly to the students' improvement. If you design the activities well, then the groups can work independently of you, so you can spend more time with a specific group or with an individual.

**Figure 5.3. Class Learning Gap Groups and Activities Immediately After Feedback**

| Four students with all strengths. | Six students with the same "their/there are/they're" grammar learning gap. | Ten students with the same "topic sentences" learning gap. | Four students with the same "paragraph organization" learning gap. | One student with an overall organizational learning gap. |
|---|---|---|---|---|
| Read more essays in this pattern. | Individually do Internet practice; the website verifies their answers. | Individually work through practice exercises and check their answers against the answer key. | As a group, they practice arranging sentence strips to form a paragraph and explaining the purpose of each sentence. When done, they check with your sample paragraph and reasons. | Meets with you. |

This short time investment (ten to twenty minutes of classroom time) can reap big dividends as your struggling writers begin to overcome their gaps. Their "golden hour" of treatment saves them from a life of suffering from this learning gap.

# 6

# Grading in Formative Assessment Writing

As a writing teacher, you have identified standards and specified the types of writing your students will do, monitored their work, diagnosed their learning strengths and gaps, given feedback, and provided time for growth. You have built in many small wins so that students are successful in their writing. A question arises as to how to grade their writing in a formative assessment environment (Wiggins, 1998).

## Comments, No Grade

One approach is to not to give grades but to give only formative comments. When students get back a "corrected" essay, they only look at the grade and not the comments. However, if you have not given a grade but you have given comments, they will read the comments. When they read these comments they learn their strengths and learning gaps. Grades often interfere with learning in the writing process. Your comments in the various sections of a rubric serve as a call for praise or improvement.

## A Proficiency Grade

If your students, parents, or administration insist on a grade, you still have many options. One option is to give a plus (+) for above proficient papers, a check (√) for proficient papers, and comments for nonproficient papers (Figure 7.1) . Until the students reach the proficient level you do not give a letter or number grade.

**Figure 7.1. Proficiency Grading**

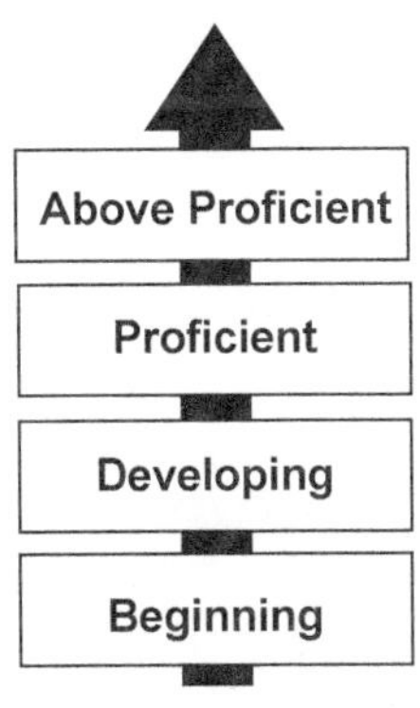

Another option involves using the state rubric scoring system with individual scores in each section, such as a "5 for Development," but you do not give an overall grade—just the score for each section. A third option is to use a proficiency coding system such as 4 (above proficient), 3 (proficient), 2 (developing), or 1 (beginning level) for each writing category or for a holistic grade.

A final option is to use the traditional 100 scale in which you impose your proficiency scoring; you enter a 30 for a 1 (beginning) work, 60 for any 2 (developing) work, an 86 for a 3 (proficient) work, and a 100 for a 4 (above proficient) work in your grade book.

When you use a scoring system, you can analyze your writers' work. You can tell which assignments they have to rewrite by looking for any grades lower than 85. Because you have these grades in a spreadsheet, you can have the computer sort from high to low to show a student's high-scoring to low-scoring papers.

## Revision Grades

When students submit a revision and you assess it as being at the proficient level or higher, then you have several choices. You can average together the original grade and the revision grade, or you can give the learners the higher grade. In a formative assessment mentality, you want students to reach a proficient or higher quality of writing, and that writing should be rewarded fully. If you do not average the grades of the original and the revision, you will focus more on student success. If you had averaged a 60 for a less-than-proficient paper with an 85 for a proficient grade on the revised paper, the student would only score a 73. Grade-conscious students may determine that there is no incentive to revise their work because if you average the two scores, their efforts do not show a substantial gain in their grade. In a formative assessment system, the student receives an 85 as he or she has reached the proficient level. In many real-life tasks, you succeed or you do not. No matter how many times a person takes a driver's test and fails it, she can still pass it. Imagine if a young driver's "failing scores" were averaged in with their passing scores; some would never get their license.

A variation on the 60, 86, 100 scoring is to give a slightly different score for rewrites. You can give all original grades as even numbers (60 = developing, 86 = proficient, 100 = above proficient) and the next lower number for the rewrite (85 = proficient and 99 = above proficient). If the students redo a 60 paper and they do it proficiently, they receive an 85, not an 86. If they redo the 60 paper to an above proficient level, they receive a 99, not a 100. Likewise if you use a proficient 1–2–3–4 scoring, you can take the score down one-tenth so a revision is 2.9 or 3.9 instead of a 3 or a 4. You can look at your grade book to determine which students received an original score of 86 and which earned a revision score of 85 on a certain type of writing. The one point difference between 85 and 86 has very minimal impact on the final grade yet allows you to analyze students' improvements.

## Cumulative Grading

Formative assessment focuses on student improvement. If students grow from essay to essay, it is not fair to count the beginning essays at the same value as the final cumulative ones. In the usual method of grading, all essays receive the same weight; each counts the same amount. For example, if students write four essays and they receive scores of 70, 75, 80 and 85, then the average is 77.5. Not only is this average score below two of the highest grades, but the averaged score does not represent the highest achievement.

The question then is how the pupils' essay scoring can reflect their writing growth. One technique is to use weighted grading with the first essay counting 10%, the next 20%, the third 30%, and the fourth 40%. Because you expect each students' essay to be better than the previous essay, you reward those improvements by weighing each essay more. Using the same four scores of 70, 75, 80, and 85, the weighted score now comes out to be 80.5.

Another technique you can consider is to take the two final highest grades and average them because they represent the two biggest improvements in writing. The average of 80 and 85 results in a score of 82.5. An even more formative approach is to award the students their final highest writing grade as their grade for writing.

The real question for you is how you reward students' growth over time.

# Section II

# Formative Assessments Within the Writing Process

This section includes actual formative assessments for prewriting, writing, and revision stages of the writing process. These follow the formative assessment approach and assume that students continually improve through the writing process (see figure below). Although the diagnosis stage of formative assessment identifies students' strengths and learning gaps, this section will focus on overcoming learning gaps.

**Constant Improvement in Writing**

A more detailed explanation of each part of the formative assessment is found in the previous chapters.

The following stages are part of each formative assessment:

- ♦ Topic
  - Identifies a specific skill in the writing process
- ♦ Information
  - Starts with some students' statements that indicate a learning gap
  - Explains the role of formative assessment in overcoming the learning gap
  - Provides students' analogies that clarify their understanding of the topic
- ♦ Monitor
  - Includes a technique to monitor this skill
- ♦ Diagnosis
  - Identifies the students' learning strength or gap
  - Identifies strategies to overcome that gap
- ♦ Feedback
  - Provides one strategy for feedback

- Time to Grow
  - Provides time for practice and growth
- Reporting Growth
  - Includes one or more ways to report student growth

As you read the assessments, you may discover that some of your views about what specifically constitutes a learning strength or gap differ from the ideas in this book. If you have a concrete measure that you and your students can readily understand, please substitute it in. Please do not use a nonmeasurable tool such as "I'll know it when I see it" or a vague tool such as "a couple of details." When you have a definite established level of proficiency, you can determine if students need additional assistance and how you can provide strategies to raise them up in the writing.

# 7

# Writing Process: Prewrite

The prewriting phase of the writing process lays the foundation for the other parts of the writing process (Figure 7.1). Therefore, students need to be assessed to verify that they have successfully completed all the parts of the prewriting phase. Formative assessment not only verifies the foundation but provides immediate help with any foundation problem.

**Figure 7.1. The Role of Prewriting in Formative Assessment**

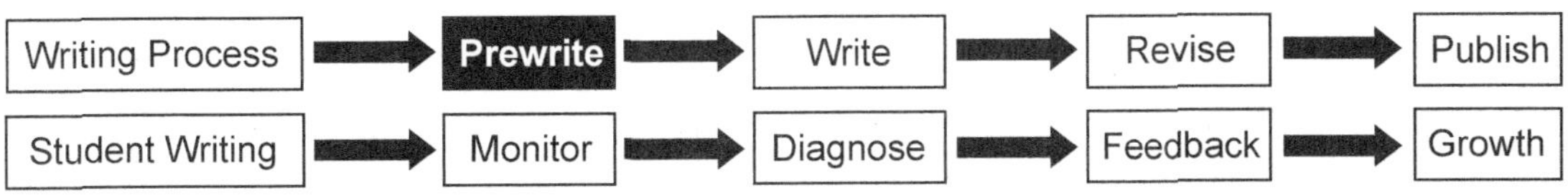


## Narrowed Topic

### Information

Students' views on narrowing down a writing topic can reveal much insight. Comments include:

- It is always somewhat difficult to narrow down the topic to specifics.
- It took effort to limit the topic to have a topic that is easy to write about.
- How to limit the topic the right way so you still have enough to write about is hard. (Figure 7.2).

**Figure 7.2. Narrowed Topic**

Formative assessment is essential at this stage to guarantee that students have a focused paper. Many pupils' papers wander aimlessly because the writers have not narrowed their topic into a manageable topic. They cannot adequately prove "war" in a few pages. For shorter essays, they have to select a limited topic that they can develop fully in a few pages. Once writers have chosen a narrowed topic, they can better determine the controlling idea for the topic. Likewise, the more concrete the topic is, the more they can focus on their supporting statements to prove it.

One student makes this analogy to explain the importance of narrowed topics: "If you put too much food in your mouth, you choke. You need to take small bites. A narrowed topic is like a small bite." Another student compares a narrowed topic to taking a picture, "I have to look at the scene and then decide which part will be the real focus of my picture."

## Monitor

Students write down the topic and then write at least three aspects, subsets, or subparts of that topic.

They identify which subtopic they will select for their writing by placing a check mark in front of it.

Students, peers, or you verify that there are at least three narrowed topics and that one has a check in front of it.

## Diagnosis

### *Identify the Students' Learning Strength or Gap*

If students generate at least three subtopics of the main topic, they demonstrate a learning strength for the skill of narrowing down a topic. When students have many narrowed topics, they have better choices for their writing. On the other hand, when students create less than three subtopics, they show that they have a learning gap in this skill.

### *Identify Strategies to Overcome That Gap*

- To help students with this learning gap, the whole group or a small group can collectively brainstorm many different subtopics out of the bigger topic. For example, for the topic of "violence" they collectively brainstorm these ideas: TV shows, movies, guns, bullying, war, gangs, domestic, school shootings, video games, and TV news coverage. The students realize that any topic can be divided into many distinct parts.
- The young writers can pair up and then individually brainstorm the same topic. For example, for the topic of "driving," Jose may identify these subparts: "permit," "freedom," "cost," "safety," "not getting a ticket," "distractions," "types of vehicles," and "weather." He has generated numerous subtopics. His partner, Selena, lists the subtopics of "being in the car," "trips," "colors," electronics," "mpg," "space," "parking," and "quality of sound."

They compare their lists. They talk to each other about which subtopic they think they can write the most about.

- These thinkers can use a graphic organizer to write the topic and then the various narrowed topics underneath it (Figure 7.3). Usually when students see empty boxes, they try to fill in as many as possible; therefore, they think of more narrowed topics. Instead of a box, you may prefer your students to use a pie-shaped graphic that has eight spaces; the students fill in the pie slices.

**Figure 7.3. Narrowed Topics**

| Topic: ______________________________ | | | |
|---|---|---|---|
| Narrowed topics: | | | |
| | | | |
| | | | |

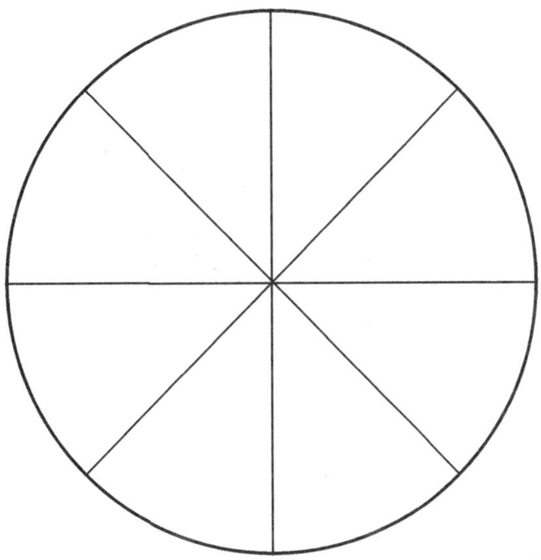

- Visual students can create a concept bubble map in which they put the topic in the first bubble and then create new bubbles underneath the first bubble for the subtopics. They may think that a subtopic still is too general so they break it down more.
- Writers can play the "make it smaller" game. In pairs, one student names a topic and the partner, says, "Make it smaller." The first student says a smaller part of the topic. If the second student thinks that the topic is still too big, he or she again says, "Make it smaller." If the first student has given a "smaller" answer, the second students says "Tell me another small part."

This cycle continues until the first student has at least three small subtopics. Then they reverse the roles.

- To generate subtopics, learners can answer questions like the following: What are numerous parts of the topic? What makes up the topic? What smaller things are connected to this topic? What are the subparts of this topic? What are some major categories within this topic?
- When the pupils explain to a peer or you why they are selecting the smaller part of the topic from their other choices, they show their logic of going from a big topic to a smaller subtopic. Peers or you can verify the logic or may ask for some clarification with statements such as "Please tell me more about your choice" or "Tell me more about how this is a smaller part of the bigger topic."

### *Feedback*

You can reassure the students that they can and do narrow down topics each day. They do not just watch a television show; they select from a wide variety of choices such as drama, comedy, reality, news, and music. They decide to wear a shirt, then they pick a specific shirt. Phrases like "Let's use the same approach in narrowing a topic" help to move the students from the perception that narrowing a topic is an unfamiliar skill to realizing they use this skill every day.

### *Time to Grow*

Most students can narrow a topic in a few minutes in the classroom. If several pupils are reducing the same topic, they grow from seeing each other's subtopics and opening their eyes to other ways of looking at the topic. Furthermore, when peers or you confirm that the writers' subtopics are really narrowed topics, then the learners feel more confident about continuing in the writing process.

### *Reporting Growth*

When students repeatedly narrow topics, they become better at doing it. After a few attempts at narrowing a topic, most students feel very comfortable in generating many narrowed topics from the original topic.

If the students or you keep a record of how many narrowed topics are generated for each topic for each writing (Figure 7.4), then the students can see growth or a high plateau in their ability to generate topics. Students can build on their past wins and know that they are capable of generating many subtopics for any given topic.

**Figure 7.4. Number of Narrowed Topics**

| Writ 1 | Writ 2 | Writ 3 | Writ 4 | Writ 5 | Writ 6 | Writ 7 | Writ 8 | Writ 9 | Writ 10 |
|---|---|---|---|---|---|---|---|---|---|
| 2 | 4 | 7 | 9 | 9 | | | | | |

# Thesis

## Information

Students identify their learning gap about writing a thesis statement with sentences such as:

- I haven't really had to focus on writing a thesis statement before.
- I had a difficult time coming up with a good thesis statement.
- I'm not direct enough when writing the thesis statement.

Formative assessment advocates the continual monitoring of students to confirm that they are progressing in the writing process. After students select a writing topic for a particular pattern of writing and narrow down the topic, they decide on their thesis statement. If these pupils do not write a solid thesis statement, then their writing begins a downward spiral. They have lost their essay before even beginning. Therefore, as soon as they have written the thesis statement, they, their peers, or you formatively assess it at this early stage of the prewriting process.

One student compares a thesis to a map with these words: "The thesis shows where you want to go. Everything has to help get you there." Another student uses a compass image because "the thesis keeps you going in the right direction. I can always check my thesis to see if I'm going to the right place."

## Monitor

The students write their thesis statements on a piece of paper. Although the writers can also say their thesis out loud, most formative assessment activities require students to see their work written down. Then they underline the topic with one line and underline the strong position (controlling idea) with two lines (Figure 7.5). If the peer reviewer does not find both of these, the reviewer writes a large question mark (?).

**Figure 7.5. Thesis Statement with Topic and Strong Position (Controlling Idea)**

All cats should be neutered.

## Diagnosis

### *Identify the Students' Learning Strength or Gap*

If students have both a topic and a strong position about the topic, then they have shown their learning strength in thesis writing.

However, when students have a learning gap in the thesis skill, they, peers, or you may not find a thesis or both critical parts of the thesis. If either part is missing, the reviewer can put a question mark above the part and write a suggestion like "Please include a strong position statement." As students self-assess, they may discover that they have a topic, but they do not have a strong position about that topic. For example, in the thesis statement of "hidden object video games are great," students discover that the narrowed topic of "hidden object video games" does not have a controlling idea such as "require much visual skill."

### *Identify Strategies to Overcome That Gap*

- The learners can read many thesis statements in which the thesis parts are identified such as

  "Americans (topic) need to spend less money (position)."

  or

  "Findit Corporation (topic) has more benefits than the ZooEnd Corporation (position)."
- The students can identify the topic and the strong position in thesis statements such as in "All cats should be neutered" and "Wii outperforms the Xbox." They can check their answers against a paper or digital answer key.
- To remember that a thesis statement has two connected parts, students can benefit from the visual metaphor of two connected objects such as in handcuffs, a bicycle, or eye glasses (Figure 7.6). One side represents the topic and the other side represents the strong position. When the students write, they have to include both aspects. They can be asked, "Did you include the handcuffs for the thesis?" or "Do you have the two parts of the bicycle to the thesis?" Likewise, a quick line drawing of handcuffs, a bicycle, or eye glasses can be a visual clue. Kinesthetic learners can use the action of bending the fingers of each hand so that the index fingers touch their thumbs and bringing the two hands together; the two hands form two connected circles.

**Figure 7.6. Eyeglass Metaphor for the Thesis**

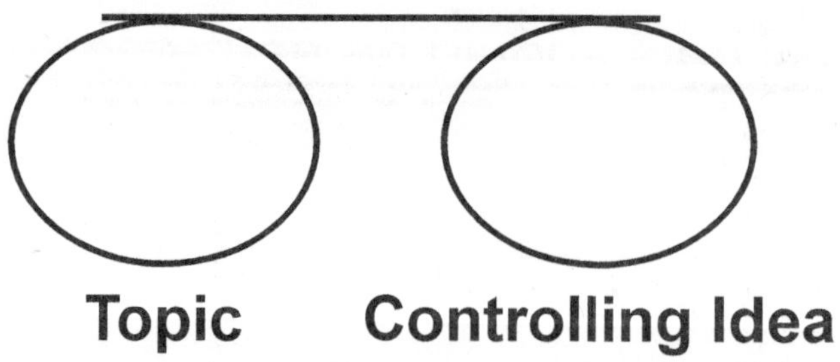


- Numerous strategies are available for those students who do not have a strong position for the topic. Some questions to ask are as follows: Would any of your friends disagree with you about this view? Would you bet your friend a quarter that you are right? Which part of the topic are you proving? What idea pushes your topic? A visual clue to help them remember to have a controlling idea is a big arrow (controlling idea) pushing a box (topic) as in Figure 7.7. The kinesthetic learner can use the index finger of one hand to push the fist of the other hand.

**Figure 7.7. Controlling Idea Pushes the Topic**

- Media-based learners improve by watching a video or an online presentation about thesis statements before they write their own. Students may view a Power Point created by you or your students that visually explains the concept of thesis. The presentation shows multiple thesis statements, some strong and some weak. The pupils identify which statements are strong and which are weak, and the slides that follow show the answers with explanations. Next, the writers have to modify the thesis statement in their own papers.
- When students use strong verbs, they have strong thesis statements. These writers can be given a starting list of strong words for each type of writing. In persuasion writing, students can use forceful words like "should," "ought to," "needs," and "has to." In compare/contrast, the writers can use powerful verbs like "outperforms," "differs from," and "produces a better...." Some key classification/definition thesis words are "consists of," "can be divided into," and "composes." The writers can substitute these or other strong verbs in their thesis statement.
- Students can write several thesis statements about the same topic. They rate each on a scale of 1 (very weak)...3 (some position)...5 (strong position). Then they select the one that best represents their strongest view of the topic. When students have to write more than one thesis statement, they look at the topic from other viewpoints and usually discover a more powerful position on the thesis.

## Feedback

You can decide if you will be direct in giving the students helpful suggestions or whether you will use an indirect approach of drawing the information out of the student. A good barometer of which technique to use is the students' learning style. If the student is an independent learner, draw information out by asking questions about their thesis. If the student is a dependent learner, try giving direct suggestions.

## Time to Grow

Build in class time so that learners can write out their thesis sentence and that they, a peer, or you can assess the thesis. Therefore, students can make instant changes, if necessary. On the other hand, if students write their thesis out of class and then continue with the writing process out of class, they could be heading off in a very nonproductive direction.

## Reporting Growth

From essay to essay, the students' theses should become stronger and more focused, moving from a possible learning gap to a learning strength. Writers need to become proficient in having both a topic and a strong controlling idea. If you indicate that the thesis is a major area of growth, then your writers will work on this area until writing thesis statements is no longer a learning gap.

You can acknowledge the changes in the students' thesis statements with comments such as "Now your controlling idea certainly gives direction to the topic!" or "Your thesis is a strong thesis; great improvement!" When young learners write a proficient thesis statement, they can draw a star next to their thesis statement.

# Idea Generation

## Information

Writers express their problems in idea generation with statements such as:

- I usually just start writing; this will take time to get used to.
- It takes time to think up ideas.
- I only have three ideas about the topic; I need many more.

After students understand the purpose of their writing, identify the topic, narrow it down, and write a thesis, they are ready to generate ideas for their paper (Figure 7.8). Ideas are words or phrases that will be used as categories, evidence, examples, or details that support the thesis of the essay.

**Figure 7.8. Idea Generation**

In the deductive writing approach, students generate and then organize their ideas (Silver, Strong, & Perini, 2007). When learners start out with few ideas, they usually end up with only a few ideas in their actual paper. Formative assessment techniques can enable students, peers, or you to assess the number of ideas generated and more importantly, provide strategies that cause an immediate increase in the number of ideas. When pupils have a wealth of ideas about a topic, they are able to write well.

A student compares idea generation to the sound of popcorn popping. Each pop is a new idea. Another student compares idea generation to a think tank where everyone is shouting out possibilities.

## Monitor

The students, peers, or you can count the number of ideas generated.

## Diagnosis

### *Identify the Students' Learning Strength or Gap*

Students who begin with at least nine ideas are off to a good start in idea generation. They show a strength in idea generation.

For a five-paragraph essay, the students will probably need to have at least eighteen ideas that can be used as evidence or examples. (Each of the three body paragraphs has at least three pieces of evidence and each piece of evidence has at least two detailed examples; a minimum of six ideas per paragraph comes to eighteen.) Although not every student will have all of these ideas in their first idea generation, they should have a majority of them. If students have less than nine, then they will probably not be able to support the thesis in a substantial manner, and they will probably have insufficient information to write the categories, evidence, and details in their essay. They have an idea generation gap.

### *Identify Strategies to Overcome That Gap*

- These young scribes learn to generate ideas by brainstorming all the words that are connected, in any way, to their topic. Depending on the number of the students with this gap, you can model this to the whole class, a small group, or to an individual. After they see the writing topic of "positive effects of a job," they say any word or phrase that they feel is connected in any way to the topic. Their answers, such as "pay," "experience," "new friends," "resume building," "something to do," "pride," "new skills," and "excuse not to do home chores," are recorded either on the chalk board or in a projected word processor. When they have said all their initial ideas, they look over the list and think for thirty seconds more. Then they volunteer any more connected ideas.

  After this modeling, the learners do their own brainstorming for another topic. When they feel they have written all the ideas down, they take a couple of deep breaths and look over their lists. Then they try to write more words.

- Another technique for students to produce many initial ideas involves a quickwrite. In a quickwrite, students write about a topic and do not stop writing for five minutes. The whole group, small group, or individual watches as you model this technique through a think aloud. They see that your pen never leaves the paper or your hands never leave the keyboard. They hear that whatever comes into your head about the topic or any other topic, you write down. They learn that you do not censor any ideas. You show that if you get a mental block, you reread what you have written. You repeat that this quickwrite is just to generate ideas; this is not writing the essay.

- Some students prefer a more visual way of producing ideas for their writing. These students who like high structure prefer to brainstorm using a well-formatted graphic organizer (Figure 7.9) that assists them in generating ideas into specific categories, evidence, and details. Other students create their own bubble concept map by adding new bubbles as they think of topics. For example, they create three large category bubbles and add smaller bubbles to each of the category bubbles.

**Figure 7.9. Graphic Organizer for Idea Generation**

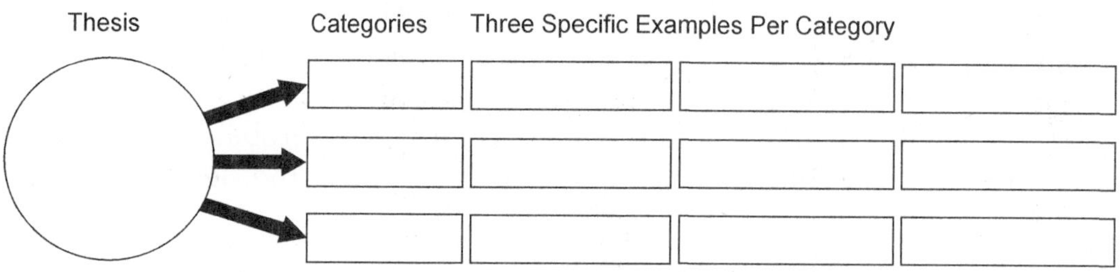


- Paired students overcome their idea generation gap by playing a verbal tag game. After the first student identifies his or her topic, he or she offers an idea about the topic. The second student offers another idea. The first student gives another idea, and the second student supplies another one. The first student writes down all the ideas. This cycle continues until neither person can think of any more ideas or until they have nine ideas. Then the second person starts his or her topic.

## Feedback

You can indicate students' strengths with statements such as "Great, you have many in-depth ideas" or the question "How do you feel about having all these ideas?" Your gentle, probing questions can help the writers to produce more ideas; you may ask "What might a friend or family member say about this topic?" or "Please share with me what might happen during...." One solution is for you to suggest that the students try a different idea-generation strategy than the present one they are using, such as a concept map or graphic organizer instead of an outline.

## Time to Grow

Although most students will have enough time in class to generate ideas and have these ideas looked over by a reviewer, the reflective thinkers may need more time. They can email their ideas to their composition buddy for her or him to look over. Another solution is for you to give some students the topic the day before so that they have time to think through ideas. Then peers or you can review their ideas in class the next day. Formative assessment affirms the immediacy of confirming whether the students have enough ideas to continue or whether they will need to generate more ideas.

## Reporting Growth

Some students like to keep track of how many ideas they can generate about a topic. They see it as a game. These pupils keep records from essay to essay. One learner has a highest-number-of-ideas score sheet in his writing journal. He keeps his present "highest idea" score until he creates even more ideas for the next writing assignment, then he crosses out the old score and replaces it with his even higher score.

When the learners hear comments like, "You have many more ideas for this essay than for your last essay" or "You generated ideas much easier this time," they have confirmation of their growth in this skill.

More importantly the students' writing should increasingly become more in-depth as they incorporate more ideas into their writing. Their papers will no longer seem to be written with surface information that they thought of at the last moment; instead their papers will have an abundance of well-thought out ideas.

# Idea Organization

## Information

Students indicate they experience some difficulties with idea organization with statements like the following:

- Not really used to preorganization.
- As I organized my ideas, I realized that many ideas did not fit, I probably would have used them in my essay without this organization.
- When I initially did my graphic organizer, I totally redid my topic and thesis after realizing I did not know what to write about.
- I should have done a more thorough job with the graphic organizer. It really helped to get my topic and essay focused.
- Once I finally organized everything, it was easy to keep on task.

Learners need confirmation that they have taken their random list of ideas and sorted those ideas into a meaningful order before they start writing. Formative assessment evaluates their organization to determine whether they are prepared to move to the next step in writing or whether they have to reorganize the ideas into a more meaningful form. Some pupils fail to organize their ideas so that their writing resembles a plate of spaghetti where the strands are thrown together; they lack organization. After writers organize their ideas, they can better assess their ideas. As learners begin to structure their ideas, they notice the parts of the essay emerge.

A student thinks of idea organization as putting together a giant puzzle with the ideas being the pieces. Each piece only fits in one spot. Another student compares idea organization to building with Legos. Not every Lego piece is used each time; only those pieces that help build the structure are used.

## Monitor

Students organize their ideas through various forms such as a list, column, outline, concept map, graphic organizer, or chart. The learners, peers, or you can determine if there is a formal organization to the ideas. The students do not just have a random collection of ideas that are scattered all over the page, but ideas have been sorted into an easily recognized order. In addition, in a more thorough inspection, the reviewer can ascertain if the organization is a logical one—do the students' ideas fit in their respective areas. Lastly, the reviewer can write a large *TH+* next to each category that definitely supports the thesis.

## Diagnosis

### *Identify the Students' Learning Strength or Gap*

Writers demonstrate this organization skill when they can take isolated ideas and group them into meaningful categories that support the thesis. For a five-paragraph essay with three body paragraphs, the students will create one category for each body paragraph that includes various pieces of evidence for each category/paragraph. However, when students lack this idea organization skill, their disconnected ideas are thrown together without any apparent logic and do not support the thesis; they have a learning gap.

### *Identify Strategies to Overcome That Gap*

- Some students benefit from starting at a basic level of sorting ideas. They can be given 3×5 cards with various terms such as "shirt," "macaroni and cheese," "England," "hamburger," "jeans," "Spain," "sweater," "China," and "pizza," to sort into categories. Once they feel comfortable sorting, then they can look at their own ideas and sort them.
- Pupils may overcome this gap by organizing all their ideas into groupings or categories. They read over the list and think of general categories. Some students like to use a numbering system for the categories; they may write "1-School," "2-Mall," and "3-Home." They look at each item in the list and write one of the three numbers in front of each item. Numerous pupils prefer to draw lines to identify the categories. They write their ideas on the left side of the paper and the major categories on the right and then draw lines

from the ideas to the categories. Other learners like to create columns and write the similar concept words in the appropriate columns. Many learners create bubble concept maps in which they draw the category bubble and then radiate out smaller ideas for each major category. Certain students make an outline.

- Many students grow in their organizational ability by understanding that their initial categories and their supporting evidence may change as they review their work. Frequently, words that are at first put in one category are moved to another category; for example, for a classification essay on motorcycles, students may move the "four engines" evidence from a "fast" category to a "sports bike" category. Also, evidence names may change as the understanding of the evidence shrinks or expands; the category "tires" may be enlarged to "wheels" to include the size of the tire and the rims. These writers can be asked to think of other bigger names for their categories. Often when students think of a bigger category name, they think of more evidence for that category.
- Students who examine their categories often find that they are missing a critical category or some critical ideas within a category. The writers can count their categories and the supporting sentences. They may discover that they only have two categories when they need three (one per body paragraph) or they may see that they only have one detail for a specific category. Some struggling writers may ask a classmate for help in thinking of more categories or evidence.
- If the writers have done a quickwrite, they can learn how to transform a quickwrite into idea organization. You can model how you move from your quickwrite (see *Idea Generation*, page 68) to organize those ideas. You underline all the ideas directly related to your topic. Then look through all the ideas and sort them into big ideas (categories), evidence, and detailed examples by labeling them with C (category), E (evidence), or D (detailed example). You pause and think about what other categories, evidence or detailed examples would prove your thesis. Next, you organize these into a graphic organizer or an outline. After this modeling of the quickwrite process, the students, individually, do their own quickwrite on a supplied topic. The pupils compare their ideas and categories in small groups. They see that there are many ways to organize ideas as long as there is a logical flow from the topic to the thesis to the categories to the evidence and to the details.
- Once the learners move from a loose collection of ideas into an outline, columns, graphic organizer, chart or concept map, they can think through the logic of their ideas. They, peers or you can determine what ideas they have and what they are missing. They can answer questions like the following: Do I have three categories? Are the categories different from one another? Does each category prove the thesis? Do the evidence and details prove the

category? Are the detailed examples very specific? Are there several details for each category? If they or a peer answers "no," then the learners can modify their idea organization.

- Some young scholars improve their thinking by playing "Which one of these does not belong?" In pairs, the students examine each other's organization to see if they can find any category or support evidence that does not belong with the others. Once a "does not belong" idea is found, the writers can change their ideas into ones that do fit or eliminate those ideas.

## Feedback

As you talk to the students at this stage, they may be frustrated at not being able to organize their ideas. After you praise the learners for the ideas that they have generated, you may pick a general category from the students' work and ask them to examine their ideas for any that might fit under that category. You may become the scribe for the students. As the students respond, you can affirm or ask for more clarification. When they are finished, praise the students for the new organization of the ideas. This "sandwich" approach of feedback (praise—criticism—praise) encourages growth rather than failure.

## Time for Growth

The time for students' growth is just after they have finished their initial organization. You schedule in-class time for the students, a peer reviewer, or you to assess their idea organization. There is an urgency of making sure that students have a logical organization before they proceed. The sooner that students receive feedback that moves them forward, the sooner they can redirect themselves before they become fixed in ineffective thinking. You can also schedule time immediately after this assessment for students to implement their new idea organization strategy.

## Reporting Growth

When these writers have done several idea generations and idea organizations, they should be able to generate and organize their ideas into easily understandable graphic organizers, charts, outlines, or concept maps. As they do this idea organization for each essay, their idea organization will become more complete. Their ideas go from a mere word or a short phrase to a long phrase or a sentence that fully expresses their ideas. With more complete ideas, they will make better choices about how to arrange their ideas to write an effective essay.

You comment on their growth by saying or writing comments like "Now, I can understand the organization of your ideas; good job" or "Last time I had some problems in seeing your organization; you have made major improvements since then."

# 8

# Writing Process: Writing

In the writing phrase of the writing process, the students actually write their essay (Figure 8.1). They take their topic, their narrowed topic, their idea generation, and their organized ideas and transform these into a purposeful essay. With formative assessment, students are continually monitored, diagnosed, and given feedback so they grow in the writing skills required in the writing phase of the writing experience. Formative assessment enables all students to do well in their writing.

**Figure 8.1. The Role of Writing in the Formative Assessment Process**

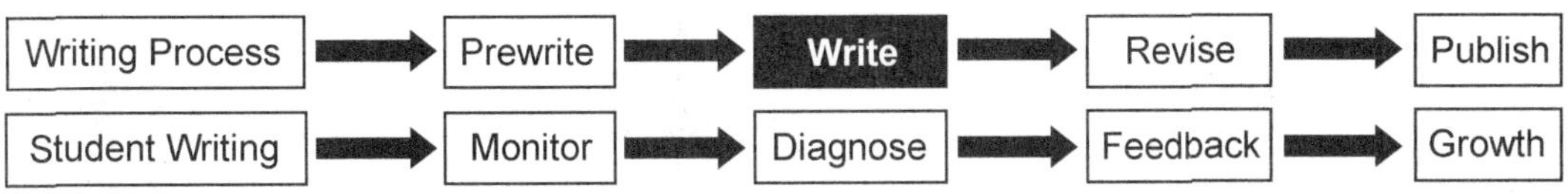


This section includes these formative assessments:

- Paragraph and Essay Structure/Formula
- Topic sentence
- Evidence
- Detailed examples
- Sequence–Transitions
- Vocabulary
- Sentence variety
- Introductory Paragraph
- Concluding Paragraph

## Paragraph and Essay Structure

### Information

Students reveal that they struggle with their essay writing structure in statements such as "I have no idea of how to organize my writing"; "Not another type of essay to figure out!"; "This type of writing is very different than what I'm used to"; and "This writing requires discipline; I'm used to writing free form."

Small writing wins accumulate to become a giant win. Formative assessment confirms each win as it takes place in the classroom. When students start writing, they want to be sure that they are following an appropriate paragraph or essay structure. They, peers, or you monitor, diagnose, and give feedback to provide them with the "green flag" to continue their writing journey. If the students get a "warning flag," they know that once they perform the formative feedback to overcome this learning gap, they will be ready again to drive to success. When students realize that most types of academic writing actually follow the same formula, they have the scaffolding they need to become better writers.

A student has the image of structure as a set of instructions that tell him how to build a model plane; the essay structure tells the steps in building an essay. Another student compares the structure of an essay to ordering online. She has to answer each question in sequence to be able to order her product.

## Monitor

Students' effective writing reveals a pattern of organization. As students write a paragraph and an essay; they, peers, or you can observe for the pattern. Students, peers, or you can label each paragraph and each sentence with its role in the pattern. Then the reviewer can compare that pattern to the usual pattern for the paragraph or the essay: a topic sentence, several pieces of evidence, and detailed examples for each piece of evidence (Figure 8.2).

**Figure 8.2. Pattern for Paragraph Success**

Paragraph = Topic Sentence + Evidence + Detailed Examples

## Diagnosis

### *Identify the Students' Learning Strength or Gap*

These young writers show their learning strength in using a writing structure when the students, peers, or you can easily follow the structure of the paragraph or essay. The students' writing will show a 90% consistency with the usual pattern for paragraph success (Figure 8.2). Likewise, the reviewers can easily identify the purpose of each sentence in the structure. Meanwhile, students who do not closely follow a paragraph or essay structure display a structure learning gap.

Because the young writers are supposed to be following a specific structure, they, peers, or you can easily determine if they are in fact following it. For example, a reviewer can read a student's paragraph and compare its structure to the pattern for paragraph success. Does it follow the following pattern?

- Topic sentence
- First evidence, one more detailed examples
- Second evidence, one or more detailed examples
- Third evidence, one or more detailed examples, conclusion

If not, what has been added or what is missing? Likewise, does the essay start with an introductory paragraph?

## *Identify Strategies to Overcome This Gap*

- As a whole group, small groups, or individual learning gap groups, students identify the TV shows they watch each week. Then several students are asked to tell what happens each week on their favorite show. A student describes the *House* TV medical show as one in which a patient comes in sick; the doctors try to treat the patient; the patient gets worse; the doctors treat the patient more; the patient becomes sicker; the patient is near death; and finally, Dr. House figures out how to cure the patient. Every week the same basic formula unfolds; the creativity is in how the story unfolds. They are asked to write out the formula for another TV show that they watch regularly. They become aware that the shows do follow a set formula; they learn that their writing can follow a set formula for each type of writing.
- The learners look at an outline of a paragraph format (Figure 8.3). This paragraph format works in each type of academic writing with minor variations. The students use their hand as a metaphor for the paragraph; they trace it on a piece of paper and then label each paragraph part (Figure 8.4). Their thumb is the topic sentence, each of the three middle fingers represent the three pieces of evidence, and the pinkie symbolizes the concluding sentence. In the hand metaphor, each of the three middle fingers has three sections so students can add up to three detailed examples for each piece of evidence. They can always check their paragraphs against their hand to affirm that they are following the paragraph structure.

**Figure 8.3. Paragraph Formula**

- Paragraph
- Topic sentence
- 1st evidence with detailed example(s)
- 2nd evidence with detailed example(s)
- 3rd evidence with detailed example(s)
- Concluding sentence

**Figure 8.4. Hand as Feedback for a Paragraph**

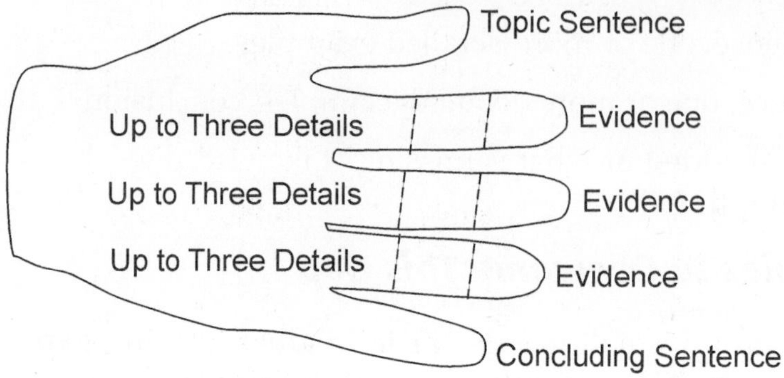


- The pupils identify the key paragraph elements (topic sentence, evidence, details, and concluding sentence) in a given paragraph. For example, they read the "carpal tunnel" paragraph (Figure 8.5). They label the purpose of each sentence at the end of the sentence with a T (*topic sentence*), E (*evidence*), D (*detailed example*), or C (*concluding sentence*). Not all paragraphs may have a concluding sentence. They can review their answers as a group or individually. Another technique is for students to use multiple highlighters to code the sentences, such as red for the topic sentence, yellow for evidence, green for detailed examples, orange for transitions (yellow and red together), and black for concluding sentences (green and red together).
- The writers with this learning gap can look at a fill-in-the-blank paragraph for an argument paragraph (Figure 8.6). They can clearly see the sentence types. Next, they can complete the paragraph and check it against a paper or digital copy.
- Certain pupils prefer a more physical activity to identify the purpose of each sentence. Individual students receive numerous slips of paper; each slip contains an individual sentence from a well-written paragraph from a previous student's essay. Each student rearranges the sentences to be a paragraph. Then, two individuals form a small group. The person with the darker-colored shirt explains the purpose of each sentence as he or she has positioned it in the paragraph. After the explanation, the second student either agrees or disagrees with each sentence position and explains his or her reasoning. Here are some sentence strips for a paragraph:
  - Meanwhile, a cottage often has three bedrooms and one bathroom.
  - Perhaps the person imagines a summer home as a deluxe mansion, a cottage, or a shack.

### Figure 8.5. Formula Paragraph: Label the Purpose of Each Sentence

Carpal tunnel syndrome has many causes ( ). People who do the same repetitive motion at work can easily develop this condition ( ). When a worker constantly has to twist something such as the top of a container, she becomes a likely candidate for carpal tunnel ( ). Likewise, as a man has to touch each product as it goes by on the production line, he increases his chances of having this condition ( ). Furthermore, when a secretary word processes many forms, this person develops a high potential for this painful medical condition ( ). Secondly, when people do the same motion over and over again during their leisure, they risk the health of their hands ( ). A young boy who strums for hours on his guitar develops a high likelihood of getting carpal tunnel ( ). Similarly, a woman who knits sweaters does the same physical motion over and over may be damaging her hands ( ). In addition, a man who paints pictures on a daily basis risks getting this condition ( ). Finally, several nervous conditions can lead to carpal tunnel ( ). A man who constantly taps his fingers on a surface repeats the same motion over and over ( ). In addition, a young girl who continually twirls her hair becomes a candidate for carpal tunnel ( ). Also, a young man who texts on his cell phone risks the health of his hands ( ). Once people know what causes carpal tunnel, they can reduce the repetitive motion and improve their health ( ).

Answer Key: *Topic Sentence, Evidence, Detailed Example, Detailed Example, Detailed Example, Evidence, Detailed Example, Detailed Example, Detailed Example, Evidence, Detailed Example, Detailed Example, Detailed Example, Conclusion*

### Figure 8.6. Fill-in-the-Blank Paragraph (Partial Example)

Complete the paragraph. Notice that the type of sentence to be inserted comes after the blanks.

______________________ (*topic*) should ______________________________

__________________________________________________________________

(*state your position in this topic sentence*). ___________________________

_______________________________ (*give your first evidence*). For example,

__________________________________________________________________

_____________________________________________________________ (*a detailed example*). In addition, ________________________________________

_________________________________________ (*another detailed example*).

_________________________________________________________________.

A second reason consists of ______________________________________

_________________________________________________________ (*give your second evidence*). For instance, _____________________________________

_____________________________________________ (*a detailed example*).

- These large summer homes comfortably sleep twenty or more people.
- Some people own deluxe mansions that have four or more bedrooms and two or more bathrooms.
- When a person thinks of a "summer home," what picture forms in the person's mind?
- Because of their size, they often cover many acres.

♦ After students can identify the formula in a paragraph, they look at the formula for an essay (Figure 8.7). Most academic writing (argument, illustration, cause and effect, compare and contrast, definition/classification, and research) use this formula. By using this structure, the writers can focus on how to express their ideas well instead of trying to struggle with the structure for an essay. They can be creative in how they express each part. As one student says, "This style of writing, classification, is very formulaic. I could see the exact format that the paper needed."

♦ To learn the structure for an essay, the students identify the purpose of each paragraph in a given essay. They write "introduction," "body," or "conclusion" next to each paragraph. Likewise, they explain the purpose of each sentence within the paragraph by labeling it. They can verify their answers by checking an in-class binder or a page of the class wiki.

♦ Struggling writers may be eased into understanding the structure by doing a modified cloze activity. They see a paragraph or essay which is missing numerous sentences such as a topic sentence, a piece of evidence, several details, a conclusion, and an attention getter. They select from a list of sentences the appropriate sentence that goes in a missing position in the essay; they explain the purpose of each sentence in the structure of the essay. They can verify their answers with your paper or digital answer key. You can quickly create this activity by opening a digitally submitted paper from a previous student, taking out a critical sentence and putting it at the bottom, replacing the removed sentence with a small blank, and removing more critical sentences. You number the removed sentences which are at the bottom so the students write the number of the sentence in the blank instead of rewriting it.

## Figure 8.7. Essay Formula

- Introductory Paragraph
  - Attention grabber
  - Thesis statement (topic and position)
- Body

**1st body paragraph**

  - Topic sentence
    - 1st evidence with detailed example(s)
    - 2nd evidence with detailed example(s)
    - 3rd evidence with detailed example(s)
  - Concluding sentence

**2nd body paragraph**

  - Topic sentence
    - 1st evidence with detailed example(s)
    - 2nd evidence with detailed example(s)
    - 3rd evidence with detailed example(s)
  - Concluding sentence

**3rd body paragraph**

  - Topic sentence
    - 1st evidence with detailed example(s)
    - 2nd evidence with detailed example(s)
    - 3rd evidence with detailed example(s)
  - Concluding sentence
- Concluding paragraph
  - Restate/paraphrase the thesis and major categories
  - Extend the idea out

♦ If writers are unsure of their structure as they are writing, they can self-check to see if they are following the paragraph or essay structure. They can place a check in front of each item in the paragraph or essay structure list as they confirm that they have it (Figure 8.8). If they discover that they are not using the structure, they can modify their writing. As they see that they are following the structure correctly, they become more confident in their writing.

**Figure 8.8. Classification Essay Formula Checklist**

| **Introductory Paragraph**<br>Attention Getter<br>Thesis | | |
|---|---|---|
| **Body** | | |
| First classification<br>__ Topic sentence | | __ First characteristic and detailed example<br>__ Transition word<br>__ Second characteristic and detailed example<br>__ Transition word<br>__ Third characteristic and detailed example<br>__ Transition word<br>__ Fourth characteristic and detailed example |
| Second classification<br>__ Topic sentence | | __ First characteristic and detailed example<br>__ Transition word<br>__ Second characteristic and detailed example<br>__ Transition word<br>__ Third characteristic and detailed example<br>__ Transition word<br>__ Fourth characteristic and detailed example |
| Third classification<br>__Topic sentence | | __ First characteristic and detailed example<br>__ Transition word<br>__ Second characteristic and detailed example<br>__ Transition word<br>__ Third characteristic and detailed example<br>__ Transition word<br>__ Fourth characteristic and detailed example |
| **Concluding Paragraph**<br>__ Paraphrase of the thesis<br>__ Major categories of proof<br>__ Extender | | |

♦ Many struggling students grow from reading an essay that exemplifies the structure of that particular type of writing. For example, students read the illustration essay (Figure 8.9) before they start to write. They think about how this writer structured the essay. As they begin to write, they can reread the sample essay to verify that they are following a similar structure.

### Figure 8.9. Essay Structure Student Exemplar

**True Love by Patrick**

Books often depict true love between a man and a woman. Does this true love only exist in books? Is true love only an imaginary love or can really people have this love? A man can show true love for his woman by paying attention, giving security, and giving material objects.

A man who truly loves his woman will give her attention. He will make sure to listen to her as she speaks. For example, when she relays her gossip about her friend Julie, he will listen attentively. Similarly, he will pay attention to her retelling the events of her school day such as the gym class. Likewise, if she mentions that she would like some help on a school project, he will volunteer. Secondly, he will give her compliments. For instance, he lets her know that her hair looks very shiny. Furthermore, he tells her that her sweater with the red stripes looks very good on her. In addition, when she gives him a soda, he says, "thank you." Lastly, he shows the woman attention by traveling to places with her, both locally and far away. He can take her to her favorite fast food restaurant, Arby's on Fridays. In another example, he asks her out to see the movie, *Valkyrie* that she has talked about. Also, he travels with her as she goes clothes shopping.

By offering and showing security, the male shows his true love for his lady. A man can pay for minor things to show his love. For example, he can pay for her ticket to the movie at the Regal Cinema. In a similar manner, when he is on the way to her house, he will stop at Dunkin' Donuts and pay two dollars and twenty-seven cents for her favorite French vanilla coffee. When they go out for ice cream at Friendly's, he pays. Additionally, the man can show security by keeping his woman safe. When they walk on the street, he walks on the street side while she walks closer to the sidewalk. Likewise, during winter, he will hold her arm as she walks over ice. Likewise, he will not open her street side car door until there is no traffic. Finally, the male can offer personal security by showing love and affection. He will let her know that he loves her by saying "I love you." Moreover, he always greets her with a warm smile showing how much he enjoys being with her. Likewise, he will use a variety of loving names for her such as "my angel," "sweetie," "beautiful one."

Lastly, the man will show his deep love by giving her material objects. He may give her flowers. For instance, he may go to the local florist and pick out some colorful flowers like dahlias for her to admire just because he loves her. In a similar vein, on their yearly anniversary, he will offer her a dozen red "Double Delight" roses. Also, on Valentine's Day he will give her some Stargazer lilies, her favorite flower. In addition, on her birthday on June 7th, he will give her a large vase of purple tulips, her second favorite flower. He will show his deep love through food for "food is the way to the heart." To celebrate their dating anniversary, the man will take her to her to Moon Buffet for her favorite sesame chicken meal. Moreover, on the weekend, he'll treat her to a picnic with her favorite roast beef sandwich from Arby's. Equally, he may bake some chocolate brownies for her. A last way of showing true love through gifts is through giving her pictures he has taken. For her birthday, he showers her with pictures of a flower garden. Furthermore, for Valentine's Day, he will give her an album of their favorite places Likewise, for Christmas, he arranges a collage of pictures he has taken of her.

Novels and fairy tales are not the only place in which true love can exist between a man and a woman. A man who truly loves a woman will show her attention, offer her security, and give her material objects. She will think of him as her "Prince Charming" as he thinks of her as his "Princess." They can live their fairy tale love here in the real world.

## Feedback

The structure for academic writing is very different than what students have done in primary and intermediate grades where they have done mostly narrative and self-expressive writing. You will acknowledge that academic writing can be a challenge at first and will assure the students that they can be successful in it. If you show students that they can incorporate some of the narrative aspects such as strong details and a singular purpose into academic writing, then they do not feel that they are starting at the bottom of their new writing. Furthermore, when you have them read an exemplar from a previous student, they realize that other students have done this style of writing successfully. Likewise, you affirm that they can use this exemplary essay as a guide for their own essay whenever they feel lost in this new structure.

## Time for Growth

Most students write several academic essays before they begin to feel comfortable with the academic writing structure. If you ask your pupils to check their writing against the formula at various times during each writing process, your writers will feel comfortable that they are following the formula and that they are growing in using the formula. As you build in class time for the mini-assessments and for implementing the new strategy after each aspect of the writing stage, the learners have time to grow.

## Reporting Growth

After they write their first essay draft, students identify the parts of their essay according to the formula. After they have practiced with this approach, most students notice a major difference in their essays. Their writing has more organization to it, and the ideas flow better. They have improved in proving or explaining their thesis through structured evidence and detailed examples.

You can positively comment on this growth with statements like "Good essay organization, your ideas flow" and "As a reader, I can easily follow your thinking about this topic because you use an essay structure."

# Topic Sentences

## Information

Not all students feel comfortable with writing topic sentences as revealed by statements such as:

- I found it difficult to keep having to look back at the thesis and tie each topic sentence to it.
- I'm not sure all of my topic statements are focused on the thesis.
- I lost focus and did not start my last two paragraphs with a topic sentence; now I know why I had so many problem in writing those two.

When students, peers, or you formatively assess topic sentences, they verify that there is a topic sentence, that the topic sentence has a topic and a controlling idea, and that the topic sentence supports the thesis. The reviewer assesses these topic sentences before the students write their paragraphs. By assessing at this point, the students have a higher likelihood that they will be successful in their writing. Unfortunately, certain students jump into a paragraph without providing a topic sentence. For the thesis of "Teen violence can be prevented by limiting media," a youth starts a paragraph with a long description of a video game or with a vague statement such as "Video games have been around for over thirty years." The reader has no sense of the direction of the paragraph. Just as the thesis statement controls all the ideas in the paper, the topic sentence controls all the ideas in the paragraph. The topic sentence provides the glue for the paragraph.

**Figure 8.10. Topic Sentences**

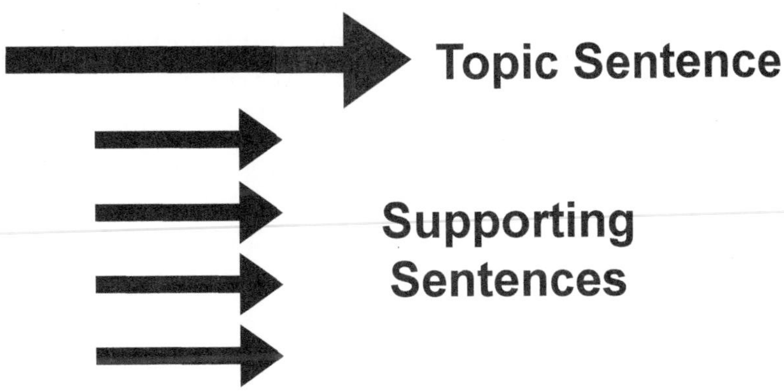


One student compares a topic sentence to a quarterback who calls a play. Once the play is called, the rest of the team follows the play. Another student thinks of a topic sentence as a teen walking many dogs. He does not let any dog wander off; he keeps all the dogs together going where he wants them to go. He leads them.

## Monitor

Students, peers, or teachers can assess topic sentences at any stage of the writing process. First, they identify a topic sentence by labeling it with *TS*. Then, they underline the topic with one line and underline the controlling idea with a double line. Next, they check the topic sentence against the thesis to confirm that the topic sentence does support the thesis; if it matches, they write *TH+*.

## Diagnosis

### *Identify the Students' Learning Strength or Gap*

Writers who have topic sentences, both a topic and a controlling idea about the topic in each topic sentence, and a match between the topic sentence and the thesis demonstrate a learning strength.

Conversely, reviewers can discover a learning gap when they realize that there is no topic sentence, the topic sentence lacks a topic or a controlling idea, or the topic sentence does not support the thesis.

### *Identify Strategies to Overcome That Gap*

- Students can read a thesis statement and then check off the supporting topic sentences of body paragraphs from a list of sentences that include topic sentences, evidence, and details. You can prepare this activity by taking a student's essay in electronic form, pulling out the thesis, and then pulling out numerous types of sentences such as topic sentences, evidence, and details. You then eliminate all other sentences.

- One strategy for overcoming this gap involves the learners writing some topic sentences for a thesis when they are given the ideas. For example, for the thesis of "All Americans should drive hybrid cars," the students may be given the categories of proof "increased miles per gallon," "safer for the environment," "less dependence on foreign oil," and "less stress on the engine." Then they are to rewrite these as topic sentences. For example, they may write these topic sentences that express an opinion about the thesis: "When all new cars become hybrid, drivers will increase their miles per gallon"; "With new energy-efficient vehicles, the environment will be safer"; "People will depend less on foreign oil when they drive modern hybrid cars"; and "Engines in new hybrid cars will have less stress." Then the learners check their answers against an answer key.

- The learners can be reminded of the handcuffs, eye glasses, or bicycle metaphor for the thesis from the Thesis section. They can verify that their topic sentences have both a topic and a strong claim by labeling each part of their topic sentences.

- Students can answer questions to verify the strength of their topic sentence such as "Does your topic sentence paraphrase the thesis idea?," "Does your topic sentence directly state how this paragraph will prove the thesis?," or "How does this sentence push the thesis along?" Other structural questions to ask about the topic sentence include "Is the topic sentence the first or near the first sentence?," "Does the topic sentence have a singular focus?," "Does the topic sentence express its idea in a simple structure rather than a long complex sentence?," and "Does the topic sentence connect this paragraph to the previous one?"
- Two simple rules help many students to improve their topic sentence learning gap. *Rule 1:* Do not use is/are/was/were. *Rule 2:* After the verb, do not use any adjective. When students cannot use is/are/was/were, they use more active verbs that strengthen the sentence. "The election was great" becomes "The election changed history." Likewise, following the second rule causes students to employ a strong noun after the verb. "The Internet is great" transforms into "The Internet provides communication."
- Some students may benefit from following a pattern such as a full restating of the thesis in each topic sentence. After students write these beginnings, they can go back and substitute in synonyms so the thesis does not sound the same each time. For example, for the thesis "When all Americans drive hybrid cars, _______," they may change it to "When the American population uses gas-electric cars, _________."

## Feedback

Because students usually assume that feedback is negative, you can praise the student for each successful topic sentence with statements such as "Solid topic sentence in your first body paragraph. Also, you have both a topic and controlling idea in your second body paragraph. Your last body paragraph includes the two critical parts to a topic sentence. Good job on having topic sentences in all of three of your body paragraphs!" You specifically identify what the students does well. The abundance of praise reaffirms that your feedback really is positive. On the other hand, several praise statements and several suggestions transform in students' minds as neutral or negative feedback.

## Time to Grow

Most writers do not instantly become good topic sentence writers. They need time and practice to develop this skill. Students do grow in this skill when they, peers, or you can identify their strengths and learning gaps, there is class time for them to modify their topic sentences, and someone reviews these topic sentences. Often when students are supposed to make changes outside of class, they do not make those changes. The best student improvements happen in the classroom where the students make a change and have it reassessed. They do not wonder if they are writing good topic sentences; they know.

## Reporting Growth

Students and/or teachers may keep a chart of how many effective topic sentences students use in each essay. Hopefully, they will quickly see the number increase to and stay at one effective topic sentence per body paragraph for each essay.

You can celebrate individual, group and class success in writing topic sentences. When students can write topic sentences for each paragraph, they have reached a milestone in their writing. You may post a success list when all students have been successful in writing topic sentences. You may have all the students give themselves a pat on the back or a round of applause to celebrate their achievement.

# Evidence

## Information

Students express their learning gap in evidence with statements such as the following:

- ♦ It was hard to narrow down the topic so much.
- ♦ Getting evidence was very hard.
- ♦ Can be a little tricky to get three (pieces of) evidence that do not overlap.
- ♦ Have to make sure not to restate or have a piece of evidence be similar to another one.
- ♦ Finding evidence from the categories but still leaving room for details can be challenging for me.

By applying formative assessment to the writing process, all students receive individual feedback on each major part of the process; if they have a learning gap, they know what the gap is, have concrete suggestions for improvement, and have the time to change the gap to a strength. Once students have written their topic sentences and have thought of their evidence to support the topic sentences, they, peers or you can do a formative assessment on their evidence. Weak writers do not support their thesis or topic with evidence. They make general statements. A typical general passage may look like "Students need to recycle in school. Recycling helps make the world better. Recycling improves the world. By recycling, we keep the planet safe." The writers convey the same information in different ways without giving any evidence support.

One student thinks of a paragraph as a restaurant menu and evidence as "appetizers," "main dishes," "salads," and "drinks." The evidence indicates the general categories of food but does not provide the specific details. Another student compares a paragraph to a clothing store and the evidence as the "jeans" section of the store.

## Monitor

Students, peers or you circle all the evidence in each paragraph that the student has used to support the thesis. The reviewer counts the pieces of evidence and puts that number next to each body paragraph; for example, the reviewer counts two pieces of evidence in the first paragraph so they write *EV-2* in the left margin. A quick scan of the paper will reveal which paragraphs have sufficient evidence and which are lacking enough evidence.

A more thorough reading will reveal if the evidence reinforces the topic sentence; the reviewer writes *TS* for the evidence supporting the topic sentence and *TS?* for the evidence not supporting the topic sentence. The reviewer knows to only mark evidence as *TS* if the reviewer is absolutely certain that the evidence supports the topic sentence.

## Diagnosis

### *Identify the Students' Learning Strength or Gap*

Writers who have three pieces of evidence per body paragraph illustrate their learning strength in evidence.

Students who have fewer than three pieces of evidence per body paragraph indicate a learning gap. When these learners have only one piece of evidence in the first body paragraph, two in the second, and one in the third, they reveal that they are not fully supporting the topic.

## Identify Strategies to Overcome That Gap

- After students brainstorm the general category, they can sort out the ideas into evidence (somewhat general information) and supporting details (the most specific information). They can examine if they have three pieces of evidence for each category by creating an outline and quickly scanning down the outline (Figure 8.11).

**Figure 8.11. Evidence in a Paragraph**

Topic sentence
- Evidence
  - Detailed examples
- Evidence
  - Detailed examples
- Evidence
  - Detailed examples

- The learners can number in large print each piece of evidence (1, 2, and 3) in the essay to make sure there are three pieces of evidence in each paragraph.
- Visual learners may prefer to use a yellow highlighter to highlight each piece of evidence. They quickly scan their papers to see if they have suffi-

cient evidence. If they lack evidence, then they include more. Visual learners can be heard to say, "I need more yellow in my writing."

- A challenge for some students is to make sure each piece of evidence is very different from the other pieces of evidence The two pieces of evidence "injury" and "pain" may, in fact, be the same piece of evidence. If the wording of the pieces of evidence seem very similar, then the writer will use other words to clearly demonstrate the differences. A student can work with another student to form "evidence-busters"; they examine each other's writing to find out if the pieces of evidence are very different or the same. An "evidence-buster" assumes the all the evidence is the same unless the writer has vividly shown that the evidence is very different. If the evidence is the same, the reviewer writes "Busted" and offers some assistance in making them different.
- A willingness to widen or narrow the students' general evidence can improve the students' writing. The learners may widen the evidence of "face injuries" to "head injuries" to include the detail of "brain damage." Likewise, they may narrow a very general piece of evidence such as "injury" to be more precise such as "head injury." Students watch a teacher or student-made Power Point presentation which demonstrates evidence being widened and narrowed. Then the Power Point presents some examples for the pupils to narrow and to widen and explains the answers.
- When students reflect and ask themselves questions about their evidence they often make changes. They may ask and answer, "Does this piece of evidence prove the topic sentence?," "How?," and "How different is each piece of evidence on a scale of 1 (*not different*), 2 (*somewhat different*), and 3 (*drastically different*)?" Based on their answers, they may alter their evidence.
- When students are unable to think of more evidence, they can answer the "because" question for each category to discover additional pieces of evidence. For the topic sentence of "War causes negative effects on soldiers' mental conditions," the students ask and answer "because" three times. They then generate the evidence of "posttraumatic stress syndrome," "missing loved ones," and "fear of death."
- Some learners do not understand that evidence consists of general proof and detailed examples provide the specifics of the proof. The details provide the facts. For the topic sentence of "Censorship of media should be eliminated," the evidence of "Schools should not censor books" represents a general statement. That sentence does not indicate specific books; the specific books are the detailed examples, such as in the sentence "Some schools prohibit the *Harry Potter* books because of the witchcraft in these books." Students can practice determining whether or not a statement represents general proof (evidence) or very specific details (detailed example). They practice with a stack of 3×5 cards that have a statement on the front. After

the students make their decision as to whether it is evidence or a detailed example, they turn over the card to verify the answer. You can write these statements and answers on mail labels, print them out, and stick them onto the 3×5 cards.

### Feedback

Numerous students find it difficult to add evidence. They struggle in changing from giving very general statements to providing more concrete evidence. You can share that many students initially experience this difficulty, but that they do learn how to provide more evidence. When you acknowledge the difficulty, students do not feel that it is their personal problem. They are more willing to try to overcome the learning gap.

### Time to Grow

Supplying evidence does not come easy to many writers. When you provide in-class time for the struggling writers to grow by giving practice opportunities that can be reviewed in class, students do become better in providing evidence in their essays.

### Reporting Growth

As students write academic paper after academic paper, they become more adept at incorporating evidence. Their evidence becomes stronger. You can acknowledge when students include evidence with statements such as "Success! You support the topic with your evidence of…" and "As a reader, your evidence makes me believe your topic sentence."

You show a student one of the student's own previous academic writings to contrast the use of evidence between the previous and current writing. You can congratulate the student on her or his success. However, if you want to help students develop more introspective skills, you can ask the students to identify the differences in their use of evidence for both writings so that the writers can realize their own growth.

## Detailed Examples

### Information

Struggling writers verify that providing detailed examples is a learning gap with statements such as the following:

- ♦ Hardest for me of anything in the essay.
- ♦ Tough to get specific.
- ♦ It was difficult to break each of the evidence down into many details.
- ♦ That was the worst part about the whole essay. Coming up with several details seemed impossible.

Formative assessment moves the learners forward in their writing skills. When students, peers or you assess the detailed examples in the students' writing, the students have an opportunity to move forward instead of being stuck in their writing. For example, some students write with vague examples that never prove the topic sentence or the thesis. For the topic sentence of "Teen violence comes from movies," the evidence of "Movies contain much violence" supports the topic sentence but "People hurt each other" is too nebulous to support the topic sentence. However, a statement like "In *Kill Bill*, 'the Bride,' a world-class female assassin takes on the gang of 88" is a detailed example that names a specific movie, identifies the lead character, and a violent part of the movie.

A student compares detailed examples to the TV news, because the news provides details of who did what to whom and when. Another learner thinks of an example as Double Chocolate Delight ice cream, which is a specific type of chocolate ice cream.

## Monitor

To monitor the number of detailed examples in an essay, students, peers or you draw a box around each detailed example in a paragraph. The reviewer counts the number of detailed examples in each paragraph and writes *EX* and that number in the margin such as *EX-4*.

Also, students, peers or you can monitor the quality of each detail by rating each detail on a three-point scale: L (low) = have no or very little idea what this detail is trying to show; M (middle) = can somewhat understand/visualize it; or H (high) = everyone can easily visualize or understand exactly what this detail is trying to show.

## Diagnosis

### *Identify the Students' Learning Strength or Gap*

When students have at least one detailed example for each piece of evidence, they are starting on their way to having a learning strength. When they can supply three supporting details for each piece of evidence, they are proficient in this skill. Likewise, when they have their examples rated as *H* (for high), they are demonstrating a learning strength in specificity of details. Therefore, in a standard five-paragraph essay with three body paragraphs, the students will have a minimum of three detailed examples per body paragraph. If they include three detailed examples for each piece of evidence, then they will have nine detailed examples per paragraph for a total of twenty-seven details for the body paragraphs of their essays. However, if students do not have at least one detailed example per piece of evidence, then they have a learning gap.

Similarly, if students' detailed examples receive an *M* (medium) or *L* (low) rating, they have to develop the skill of being more specific.

## Identify Strategies to Overcome That Gap

- ♦ Often a visual clue helps the learners to realize the critical role that detailed examples provide in a paragraph (Figure 8.12). The topic sentence provides the foundation and the evidence represents the framing walls. The detailed examples are the walls and windows in the house. The students can verify if their supporting details do build up the paragraph. When students arrange their own writing (topic sentence, evidence, and details) in the same format as the graphic, they often have the epiphany that their details do not support any evidence.

**Figure 8.12. Details as Walls and Windows of a House**

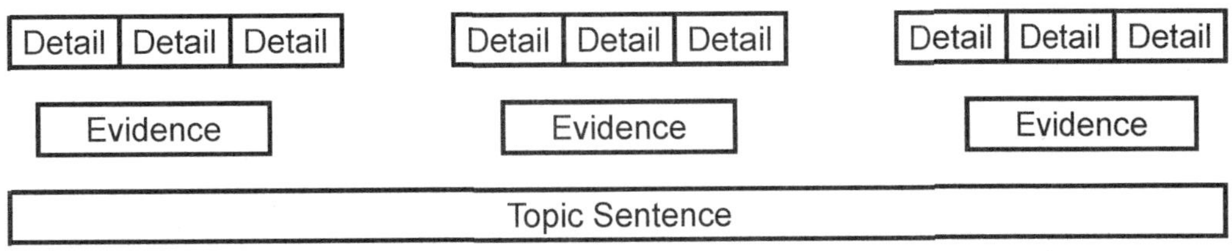


- Many students benefit from seeing the degree of specificity that academic writing requires. They can read a sample paragraph and put a box around all the details as illustrated by the following sentences: "Another classification of gaming consoles includes Sony Play Station. The superior graphics allow the gamer to see a specific tree move. This graphics machine sells for four hundred dollars. This machine is all black and stands nine inches tall." After the pupils identify the detail in each sentence, they then rewrite their details to be very specific.
- Writers with this learning gap can use the *Who-What-Where-When-For How Long/Much* approach to writing details. They can make sure that any detail includes at least two of these: who (name a specific person or group) did what (tell exactly what they did), where (name a specific place), when (tell the time, day, year), for how long/much (tell length in hours, days, years, or size, number). Students can be given a topic sentence, a piece of evidence, and then be asked to write detailed examples by using the *Who-What-Where-When-For How Long/Much* approach. For example, for the topic sentence of "Chico's restaurant attracts more customers than Pancho's because of appearance," a student may write "The outside of the two buildings shows the difference. Chico's has an artistic twenty-foot-long mural of rural Mexico over the entrance. However, Pancho's only has a five-foot orange neon sign saying 'Pancho's.'"
- These writers can improve in their detailed example gap by being given sentences with general statements that they change into specifics. For example, they can change "At night she relaxes by watching TV" to a statement that includes a specific TV show such "At night she relaxes by watching *Monk* on TV." Similarly, students change the vague "He studies for a long time" into the concrete detail of "He studies history for two hours." Students can

modify a series of these vague statements until they can provide specific details for each.

- The learners can read a topic and generate their own detailed examples. For the evidence of "Americans show their obsession with money by buying the newest technology"; students can generate a list of very specific newest technologies. They will not write a "new cell phone" (general evidence) but will identify a specific cell phone such as the "Blackberry Curve 8330." Also, they will not write "a laptop" (general evidence) but the "13-inch MacBook." One student explains, "If a person cannot search that exact term on the Web and find the item immediately, then the term is not specific enough. Evidence has to be that specific."
- As the writers think about their detailed examples, they look at the following list and place a check mark over each specific item that they use (Figure 8.13). For example, if they write "Americans buy a large riding lawn mower like the Toro Z100 when they only have a thirty-foot-by-five-foot lawn," they put a check mark over product and size. If they find they do not have check marks, then they rewrite to include the concrete detailed example.

**Figure 8.13. Specific Details Checklist**

_____ hour, day, month, season, weather, year, time period

_____ person, place/location, animal, product, object, activity, class

_____ sound, sight including colors, taste, texture/feeling, smell

_____ number, amount, size, price, distance

_____ book, magazine, song, TV show, movie, video game, website

_____ historical event, holiday, celebration, disease/illness, occupation

## Feedback

Students benefit from knowing when they do and when they do not use exact details. When students do have specific detailed examples, you give feedback that verifies that you noticed the details with statements such as "You support your ideas with many specific detailed examples such as the different movies." When peers or you notice the lack of detailed examples, the writers can be asked, "What facts can you tell me about this?" or "Can you give me a specific example of this?" In addition, you have exemplary detailed example sentences that students can compare to their own statements. You may guide the students by asking "Which of these is more specific? How? What can be done to change the less specific one to be as specific as the other?"

If students do follow a given suggestion exactly and still do not show improvement, then the students need a different strategy. If the strategy matches their learning style, then they have a greater chance of being successful.

## Time to Grow

In-class time represents the best time to grow in this skill. As students become aware of the learning gap and receive precise suggestions on how to improve, they begin their growth immediately. Their peers, you, or technology consistently verify their baby steps in improvement until they can walk in this skill.

## Reporting Growth

As soon as the students, peers, or you notice the lack of details, the growth process can begin.

You may set up a detailed example score card for the students by creating a chart with the number of details going down and the specific essays (Essay 1, Essay 2) going across (Figure 8.14). The students mark an *X* for each detail they have in the essay. As they look at their chart, they can see their success.

**Figure 8.14. Detailed Examples Over Time**

| | A | B | C | D | E | F | G | H | I | J |
|---|---|---|---|---|---|---|---|---|---|---|
| 1 | Bob T | Writing → | | | | | | | | |
| 2 | Detailed Examples ↓ | 1 | 2 | 3 | 4 | 5 | 6 | 7 | 8 | 9 |
| 3 | 1 | | | | | | | | | |
| 4 | 2 | | | | | | | | | |
| 5 | 3 | | | | | | | | | |
| 6 | 4 | | | | | | | | | |
| 7 | 5 | | | | | | | | | |
| 8 | 6 | | | | | | | | | |
| 9 | 7 | | | | | | | | | |
| 10 | 8 | | | | | | | | | |
| 11 | 9 | | | | | | | | | |
| 12 | 10 | | | | | | | | | |
| 13 | 11 | | | | | | | | | |
| 14 | 12 | | | | | | | | | |
| 15 | 13 | | | | | | | | | |
| 16 | 14 | | | | | | | | | |
| 17 | 15 | | | | | | | | | |
| 18 | 16 | | | | | | | | | |
| 19 | 17 | | | | | | | | | |
| 20 | 18 | | | | | | | | | |
| 21 | 19 | | | | | | | | | |
| 22 | 20 | | | | | | | | | |
| 23 | 21 | | | | | | | | | |
| 24 | 22 | | | | | | | | | |
| 25 | 23 | | | | | | | | | |
| 26 | 24 | | | | | | | | | |
| 27 | 25 | | | | | | | | | |
| 28 | 26 | | | | | | | | | |
| 29 | 27 | | | | | | | | | |

# Sequence–Transition Words

## Information

Many students have a transition word gap as illustrated by these statements:

- I'm not used to writing with transition words.
- I was confused at first since transition words are new to me.

- I should use (transitions) much more.
- Making them (the sentences) flow while not using the same words over again was at times difficult.

Students' improvement in writing does not happen magically. Through formative assessment, the writers become aware of a transition word learning gap, learn about a new strategy, and make changes in their writing that result in an improvement in this skill. Numerous students have this gap; they do not use transition words. When students do not use transition words or phrases, their writing lacks flow; the reader struggles to understand how the sentences are connected. Transition words can be seen as a set of directions that tell the readers when they are approaching a new road, when they are seeing sights along the same road, when they are going in a different direction and when they have arrived. Although there are more sophisticated transitions, students can start with the basic transition words.

A student compares transition words to a traffic officer who directs the drivers when to stop, when to go, and where to go. Another student compares transition words to a couple holding hands; transitions words connect two sentences just as a couple connects through holding hands.

## Monitor

Students, peers, or you can put a triangle around all the transition words in a student's writing passage or put a large *T?* in the writing to indicate where a transition would help guide the reader. The reviewer reads a passage such as "Another technology to transform a person's life is the Internet. People use the web to communicate. They text message their friends many times during the day about an upcoming exam. People send photos of their sightseeing trip in Lima, Peru to their friends back home. They use their Facebook account to keep their friends informed about their daily schedule." The reviewer puts a triangle around the transition word "another" and then inserts a *T?* before the sentences beginning "People send photos" and "They use their" to indicate that transitions are missing.

## Diagnosis

### *Identify the Students' Learning Strength or Gap*

In a paragraph that has three pieces of evidence and two detailed examples for each piece of evidence, there may be one transition word between each piece of evidence and one transition word between each detail, for a total of five transition words. When students, peers, or you identify at least four transitions words in each paragraph that guide the reader, they know that the writer has a transition learning strength. Conversely, writers with fewer than four transition words in a paragraph probably have a transition word learning gap.

## *Identify Strategies to Overcome That Gap*

- Students benefit from understanding not only that there are transition words but that there are different categories of transition words. They receive a handout with the transition words divided up by their purpose, such as transition words to show comparison and contrast, illustrations, and conclusion. Figure 8.15 illustrates contrast transition words. The learners read some sentences that use these transition words.

**Figure 8.15. Contrast Transition Words**

Contrast transition words:

| | | | | |
|---|---|---|---|---|
| however | in contrast | yet | differ/difference | instead |
| still | on the contrary | conversely | otherwise | on the other hand |
| meanwhile | nevertheless | but (do not start a sentence with "but") | | rather |

Examples:

Mercedes studies for three hours, yet Luis only studies for ten minutes.

At Chico's, the customers receive a free appetizer; however, at Pancho's, the customers pay five dollars for an appetizer.

- These struggling writers read a paragraph with the transition words underlined and then they tell what purpose each transition word serves, such as introducing a new idea or details for an idea, opposing idea or concluding idea (Figure 8.16). They can verify their answers with an answer key.

**Figure 8.16. Identify the Purpose of Underlined Transition Words**

The local store has a negative appearance when compared to the supermarket. The window are covered with grime in the local store. In contrast, the supermarket has sparkling clean windows. Similarly, electrical wires hang out of holes in the walls in the local store. Yet, the supermarket does not have any holes; it does have attractive pictures. Next, the floor of the neighborhood grocery store has many tiles missing so that a person has difficulty walking on the floor. Meanwhile, the supermarket floor has all its tiles and the tiles floor form an attractive flower design. A person tries to avoid the dirty local store but looks forward to entering the clean supermarket.

Answer Key: In contrast - Contrast; Similarly – Addition; Yet – Contrast; Next – Sequence; Meanwhile – Contrast; but – Contrast

- The students practice by inserting transition words into given sentences. For instance, in one exercise, two opposite ideas are given, such as "The first poster has two colors. ________ , the second poster has five colors." The students insert a contrast transition words chosen from a list of various transition words.

- In a sample paragraph the pupils insert the transition words from a list at the bottom as in Figure 8.17. Then they verify their answers with an answer key. Once they know that similar transition words such as contrast words can often be used interchangeably, they feel more comfortable in using transition words.

**Figure 8.17. Paragraph Missing Transition Words**

The supermarket clerks present a much more positive atmosphere than local store employees. In the corner grocery store, the workers insult the customers by calling them "idiots." ____________ the employees at the supermarket smile and greet the customers with a warm "hello." ________________ the cashiers at the local store throw the customers' change on the counter. ____________ the cashiers at the large supermarket carefully place the money in a person's hand. ____________ the employees at the neighborhood store talk on the phone and ignore the customers ______________ the employees at the supermarket ask how they can help the customer. A person feels welcomed in the supermarket and feels abused at the local store.

*Possible transition words:* in conclusion, as a result, in addition, also, furthermore, however, on the other hand, conversely

- After the writers organize their ideas in a graphic organizer, they add their transition words into the graphic organizer. Notice that Figure 8.18 includes detail transition words and contrast transition words as part of the graphic organizer. When students complete this graphic organizer by adding in the transitions, these learners can feel confident that they are guiding the reader.

**Figure 8.18. Transition Word Columns in a Contrast Essay Graphic Organizer**

| | | Detail transition words | Item 1 | Contrast transition word | Item 2 |
|---|---|---|---|---|---|
| Point-by-point contrast → | Evidence A:<br><br>Topic Sentence | <br><br>X<br><br>Also<br><br>In addition | Details:<br><br>1<br><br>2<br><br>3 | <br><br>Measurable<br><br>However<br><br>On the other hand | Details:<br><br>1<br><br>2<br><br>3 |

- ♦ As students think about their transition words, they can compare their drafts to a transition paragraph sample (Figure 8.19). As they start with the first body paragraph, they verify if they have transition words in the approximate place as in the transition sample; if so, they put a check mark in front of the word "Transition" in the sample.

**Figure 8.19. Paragraph Transitions**

Paragraph transitions
Topic sentence
1st evidence
    1st detailed example
    *Transition* 2nd detailed example
    *Transition* 3rd detailed example
*Transition*—2nd evidence
    1st detailed example
    *Transition* 2nd detailed example
    *Transition* 3rd detailed example
*Transition*—3rd evidence
    1st detailed example
    *Transition* 2nd detailed example
    *Transition* 3rd detailed example

- ♦ After students write their graphic organizer, body paragraphs, or draft, they ask their essay buddy to peer review for transition words. If there is more than one type of transition word, the reviewer makes a triangle around the transition word and adds letters such as *T C* for transition contrast word or *T D* for transition detail word. If students do not have transition words or transition phrases, then the peer reviewer indicates the absence of the transition words by writing *T?* where a transition is missing. The reviewer can provide more useful feedback by specifying the type of transition that is missing such as "Use a contrast transition word here."
- ♦ When learners compare their essays to an exemplar for the same type of writing, they identify the transition words in the exemplar by making a triangle around them and then verify that they have used similar transitions. Students see that a pattern of transition words emerges, such as a transition word before the second and third details or a contrast word between two sentences about the same evidence for two stores. They can model their transition words after the exemplar.

## Feedback

When students, peers, or you give formative feedback immediately after a writing process activity, students perceive the feedback as meaningful; the learners are more willing to make changes to improve. Likewise, when the reviewer provides ongoing feedback, the students can be constantly improving in the skill of using transition words. You may praise the student with comments such as "You have used a variety of transition words to connect the ideas in your writing. Good going!" or "As a reader, your contrast transition words made me very aware of the differences between the two restaurants."

## Time to Grow

Students often do not concentrate on improving this transition sequencing skill until they have mastered many other skills. As they begin to learn this skill, writers often require much concentrated practice. When they practice in a class where they constantly receive feedback, they do grow in the skill over time. Even though they may learn how to use certain transition words in a contrast essay, they may not have learned how to use other types of transition words. Being proficient at using transition words takes time.

## Reporting Growth

When students begin to use transitions, they express the difference it makes with statements such as the following:

- My essay sounded better afterward.
- I put in the (transition) ones that fit and it felt like my writing went together.
- When I have to put in transition words, I analyze my writing more.

You will notice a greater flow to the writers' papers and you can praise them for their achievement. "Now you connect the ideas through transitions. Thanks for guiding me through your paper with transitions" or "As a reader, I find your papers easier to understand now that you use transition words."

# Vocabulary

## Information

Many students have problems in using synonyms in their writing as evidenced by these statements:

- Could not think of many other words for the thesis topic.
- I repeated a lot, should have used more synonyms.
- Don't feel my vocabulary is big enough to come up with many synonyms.

In a formative assessment approach, you take responsibility for helping each student be successful in each aspect of writing. When students display a learning gap in vocabulary, you will not leave the improvement to chance. You select precise activities to guide the students forward in vocabulary. Certain students repeat the same key words over and over again in their writing. The reader becomes bored. The writer appears to have a primary level vocabulary because they do not use synonyms for the key words in the thesis, topic sentences, and evidence. For example, in the passage, "My dog, Ralph, is very fast. He is so fast that I cannot keep up with him. Ralph is so fast that he can catch a thrown ball before it hits the ground. He is a fast runner; he almost catches cars," the reader quickly gets tired of reading "fast."

A pupil compares poor and rich vocabulary to a baby who makes the same nonsense sound over and over, and a baby who after a few months uses real words such as "mom." Another student imagines vocabulary as the difference between an artist who only has one color with which to paint and an artist who has a whole palette of colors.

## Monitor

Students can do a class practice of an adjective vocabulary continuum line. For example, doing this activity with the words "poor" and "rich" (Figure 8.22), they add any adjectives above, below, or between "poor" or "rich" in sequential fashion. The class's list for Figure 8.20 is displayed here: "destitute...broke...*poor*... middle class...comfortable...*rich*...loaded...wealthy...." Next the students are asked to do a vocabulary opposites continuum line for "small" and "big"; they write "small" about one-third of the way down their paper and write "big" about two-thirds of the way down the paper. Then they add in as many adjectives as they can. When they are done, they count the number of words that they added.

**Figure 8.20. Poor to Rich Vocabulary Continuum Line**

.

.

poor

.

.

.

rich

.

.

## Diagnosis

### *Identify the Students' Learning Strength or Gap*

Students who have at least four valid adjectives have a start toward being strong in this writing skill. Shanelle has this list: "microscopic...*small*...tiny...little...*big*...large... overgrown...giant...enormous...gigantic." She has added eight vocabulary words.

Meanwhile, students who have added fewer than four words or who have vague words illustrate a learning gap in vocabulary. For example, Zeph creates this continuum: "small…tiny…*big*…bigger…biggest…big sized." He has added four words; however, he has three versions of "big"; also, "big sized" is not the largest of the adjectives.

## *Identify Strategies to Overcome That Gap*

- These low vocabulary learners can practice with an antonym sheet (Figure 8.21). Words in the first and second columns are opposites. The students use their "magic" index finger to cover one word in the second column. They look across to the word in the first column, say the antonym in their mind, and then pull down their finger to check. They self-check their own vocabulary.

**Figure 8.21. Antonym Practice**

| | |
|---|---|
| above | below |
| absence | presence |
| abundance | lack |
| to accept | to refuse |
| accidental | intentional |
| active | lazy |
| to add | to subtract |
| to admit | to deny |
| advanced | elementary |
| afraid | brave |

*Source:* Reprinted from englisch-hilfen.de (http://www.englisch-hilfen.de/en/words/opposites2.htm) with permission.

- The young learners can practice individually with synonyms in a manner that does not hurt their delicate self-esteem. When they receive this partial listing from a synonym handout (Figure 8.22), they fold the paper in half horizontally so they only see Side A. The learners look at the word on the left side and write out as many synonyms as they can for the given word. Then they continue down the left column to the next word until they have done the whole left side. Next, they unfold the sheet to check their synonyms against those on the sheet.

**Figure 8.22. Synonym Practice**

| Side A | Side B |
|---|---|
| sad | unhappy, downcast, gloomy, depressed, melancholy, blue, dreary, discouraging |
| stop | hinder, impede, obstruct, check, block, thwart, hamper, intercept, prohibit, stall, slow down |
| home | residence, habitation, abode, lodging, dwelling, quarters, domicile, shelter |

- The learners with this learning gap read the paragraph about the dog (Figure 8.23). They quickly observe that the writer uses "fast" many times. They brainstorm synonyms for "fast." After a minute, they share their lists. Then they substitute the synonyms for the repeated word. By double-spacing the paragraph, the students can easily cross out "fast" and write a synonym above the repeated word.

**Figure 8.23. Synonym Substitution**

Ralph, Tom's dog, is very fast. He is so fast that I cannot keep up with him. Ralph is so fast that he can catch a thrown ball before it hits the ground. He is a fast runner; he almost catches cars.

- Students write out their thesis and underline the key words in the thesis. Then, they write synonyms underneath each of the key words. Good writers do not repeat the same thesis words in their writing; they use synonyms. For example, if students are writing an illustration essay with the thesis of "the causes of a horrible party," they can identify synonyms for "causes," "horrible," and "party." For "horrible," they may use "terrible" in one sentence, "disgusting" in the next, "dreadful" in the subsequent, and "pitiful" in the last sentence. Often when pupils think of synonyms, they realize that their original word does not convey what they wanted. For example, one learner writes "the causes of a bad accident" but as she looks for synonyms for "bad," she realizes that her synonyms for "bad" do not convey her original idea. She changes "bad" to "tragic." Certain writers like to create columns of synonyms so that they can look at the list whenever they need an alternative word (Figure 8.24).

**Figure 8.24. Synonyms Columns**

| *Causes* – Synonyms | *Horrible* – Synonyms | *Party* – Synonyms |
|---|---|---|
| conditions | terrible | event |
| reasons | disgusting | gathering |
| circumstances | dreadful | celebration |
| | pitiful | get together |

- During the peer-review of a draft, students play a game called "Find Repeats." Students look through their partner's paper to see how many times the same critical word(s) is(are) repeated. They especially look for the key words from the thesis, category or evidence. When they find a word repeated more than twice, they circle it and write *Synonym?*. The authors can look up the synonyms in a printed thesaurus, in their word processor's thesaurus, or in an online thesaurus such as thesaurus.com (http://thesaurus.reference.com).

## Feedback

When you invite the students to think of what other words there may be for a certain word, you encourage their use of synonyms. As you read their draft, you can highlight several of the synonyms for the same word and write "Good use of synonyms for…" or "As a reader, I appreciate your variety of words for…; your reading is more interesting."

## Time to Grow

If you give students in-class time to write out synonyms as soon as they have written their thesis, categories, and evidence, you greatly increase their use of synonyms in the essay. When they start out with a list of synonyms in the prewrite phase, they are more likely to put these in the paper.

## Reporting Growth

When students use synonyms in their writing, they notice the changes. They understand that their writing goes from a repetitive use of the same word to many different words for the original word. Some pupils like to boast about their use of synonyms with statements such as "I'm up to five synonyms for my thesis word!" You can ask the learners to comment on their improved use of synonyms in their essay. As they either say or write their own observations, you can confirm that you too have noticed the change.

# Sentence Variety

## Information

This learning gap is revealed in student statements such as the following:

- I write all my sentences the same way.
- My teachers talked about it but I didn't get it.
- It's hard to think about variety when you're thinking about arguing your topic.

Continual improvement constitutes an essential part of formative assessment. If students do not know that they have a learning gap in sentence variety, they will never improve. Formative assessment provides students with the strategies to grow in their skill of sentence variety . Unfortunately, "Many students lack sentence variety. Many students write the same type of sentence. Many students keep the same word order." This quotation illustrates the sentence variety gap that makes students' writing very boring. Such writing has an elementary tone to it.

A student thinks of sentence variety as a spy who wears many different disguises; the same person can look very different. Another writer imagines sentence variety as a young girl's wardrobe: She can wear a different outfit each day or she can wear the same blue blouse and same blue jeans every day.

## Monitor

One quick technique for monitoring the length of sentences is for students, peers, or you to count the number of words in each sentence and list that number down the margin such as "7, 8, 8, 7."

The reviewer highlights with a blue highlighter the first three words of each sentence, reads over the three words, and puts a large plus sign (+) each time a sentence starts with a new beginning and a large dash (–) when the sentence starts in the same way that a previous sentence has. A quick scan of the paper reveals if sentences begin in different ways.

In addition, the reviewer can check for the various patterns in each sentence. This reviewer can identify the order of the words such as subject, verb, direct object, and prepositional phase and observe if the other sentences follow this exact same pattern.

## Diagnosis

### *Identify the Students' Learning Strength or Gap*

When students write more than fifty percent of their sentences of varying word length, with different beginnings, and with different sentence patterns, they have the learning strength of sentence variety.

However, when students write more than fifty percent of their sentences with the same number of words, with the same beginnings, and with the same sentence pattern, they exhibit this learning gap. Often students will have a different beginning but still have the same sentence pattern such as "The boys practice with their friend. The buddies work with him."

## *Identify Strategies to Overcome That Gap*

- The writers can read several exemplary paragraphs that have varied writing. They can contrast each sentence in terms of length, beginning, and pattern. These pupils can count the number of words in each sentence. In addition, they will highlight the first three words in each sentence to confirm that they start differently. Furthermore, they check the sentence pattern to see the ways in which it varies. The learners compare this paragraph to their body paragraphs.
- Some students benefit from contrasting two paragraphs: one which has varied sentences and one which does not have varied sentences. They can indicate the differences between the two paragraphs and then compare their analysis with your digital or paper answer analysis.
- Writing varied sentences can become a game when the students roll a dice. For the low numbers of one or two, the pupils write a sentence of two to five words; for a roll of three or four, they write a sentence of six to twelve words; and for a roll of five or six, they write a sentence of more than twelve words. After students play this game a few times, they realize that they can vary the length and complexity of their sentences.
- These learners can rewrite a paragraph which does not have varied sentences into one with varied sentences. To facilitate this exercise, you can create a two-column chart; you lay out a nonvaried paragraph sentence by sentence in the left column, and in the right column you provide spaces for the students to rewrite each sentence. Because the two paragraphs are side by side, the students can better comprehend the changes they have made.
- To affirm that they have used a variety of ways to start their sentences, the students can check their own writing for the use of the following sentence starting techniques (Figure 8.25). They put one plus sign (+) in front of each variety for each time that they have used it. For example, if they have started four sentences with adjectives, then they write four plus signs in front of "Adjective."

**Figure 8.25. Sentence Starter Checklist**

_____ *Adjective:* Sincere students use different types of sentences.

_____ *Transition word:* After reviewing other writing, students use different types of sentences.

_____ *Infinitive (to + verb):* To write well, students use different types of sentences.

_____ *Gerund (verb + ing):* Writing well requires that students use different types of sentences.

_____ *Past-tense verb (verb + ed):* Determined students use different types of sentences.

_____ *Dependent clauses:* When they think, students use different types of sentences.

_____ *Adverb:* Seriously written essays have different types of sentences.

_____ *A common noun:* Students use different types of sentences.

♦ Words or phrases on 3×5 cards provide practice for changing the pattern of a sentence. Students receive a packet of words or phrases that are written individually on 3×5 cards; there are cards for the subject, verb, direct object, prepositional phrase, dependent clause, transition word, etc. The students arrange these cards to create a meaningful sentence. Then they rearrange the words; they may have to add new words. For example, they have the following words/phrases: "the tall man," "exercises," "by playing," "basketball," and "for three hours"

The learners might rearrange these words/phrases into these patterns:

- For three hours, the tall man exercises by playing basketball.
- Playing basketball for three hours provides exercise for the tall man.
- In order to exercise, the tall man plays basketball for three hours.
- Basketball playing gives the tall man three hours of exercise.

After doing this exercise, students rearrange the order of some of their sentences.

## Feedback

Because sentence variety includes three distinct aspects (length, beginning, and pattern), you can find many opportunities to congratulate the students on their strengths and to provide strategies for their learning gaps. To encourage the students to be lifelong self-assessors, the peer or you can listen as the students do their own self-assessment and tell which new strategy they used as a tool for improvement and how well it has worked. The reviewer becomes more of a sounding board and verifier than a person giving directions.

## Time to Grow

Over many years of writings, students have developed their present habits of writing. Changing habits take time. You have to bring the new habits to the front of the students' attention for many times for a change to take place. When you provide in-class time for improvement in sentence variety, there is a very high chance that the change will take place. Through the students' self examination, peer review and your review, the student can be scaffolded to change the habit.

## Reporting Growth

Students who at the beginning of their writing had more than 50% of their sentences of the same general length and structure and greater than 50% starting with the same words can measure their success as they vary their sentence length, vary their sentence structure, and have a greater variety of sentence beginnings. The logical/mathematical pupils may keep a chart of their numerical changes. Many other students can instantly identify the drastic difference in their writing by just rereading their most recent essay.

You can comment when the students have shown strength in this skill by writing or saying comments like "Drastic improvement in your sentence variety from your beginning writing! Continue to use variety." and "As a reader, I find your sentences more varied than previously."

# Introductory Paragraph

## Information

Students express that writing introductory paragraphs is not easy with statements such as the following:

- ♦ Can be difficult for me to write an intro paragraph.
- ♦ Couldn't come up with a good attention getter.
- ♦ It was tough coming up with a hook that fit my thesis.
- ♦ Finding how much to write in the attention getter and thesis was hard.

Some students get stuck in their writing of introductory paragraphs; they spin their wheels without moving. In each essay, they display the same learning gap; they do not show any progress. Formative assessment enables these struggling writers to get traction through a new strategy to move forward. As soon as the students write an introductory paragraph, they, a peer, or you formatively assesses it. The young writers know instantly if they are still stuck and, if they are, they immediately receive feedback to help them improve. For example, many students fail to use an introduction that interests the reader in the topic. Others jump directly into the thesis and the reader feels like she/he is joining the second half of a TV show. Also, some students do not include a thesis in the introduction so the reader does not understand the purpose of the essay.

One student feels that an introductory paragraph is like a person meeting another person for the first time—if one person is boring, then the other person wants to leave immediately. Another student thinks of an introductory paragraph like a text message about a party—it has to tell enough to get the person interested in the party.

## Monitor

- Students, peers, or you can label the attention grabber with a large exclamation mark (*!*) and write *TH* next to the thesis statement.
- Then they can rate the attention grabber as to how interesting it is on a 1 to 5 scale, where 1 = no interest or plain, 3 = some interest, and 5 = very interesting or dramatic.
- Next, they can label the students' attention grabber technique by writing *SS* (a startling statement), *Q* (a quotation), *A* (an anecdote or very short story), *?* (a question), *M* (metaphor or simile), or *O* (other attention-getter strategy of ______).
- The reviewer can label the two parts of the thesis by underlining the topic and double underlining the strong position about the topic.

## Diagnosis

### *Identify the Students' Learning Strength or Gap*

If the students' writing has been labeled with an exclamation point or a *TH*, they have a solid introductory paragraph, which is a learning strength.

If students do not have an attention getter or their attention getter is not compelling (less than a 4 on the interest scale), or if they do not have a thesis statement or do not have the topic and the controlling idea of the thesis statement, then the students demonstrate a learning gap for introductory paragraphs. These students will have to implement new strategies to be successful introductory paragraph writers.

### *Identify Strategies to Overcome That Gap*

- Struggling writers profit from identifying the two elements of an introductory paragraph in various examples. As they read the paragraphs, they label the attention grabber with a large exclamation point (*!*) and they label the thesis with a large *TH*. They can verify their answers with your paper or digital answer key.
- To improve in their attention-getting skills, these writers read a thesis statement and then read several different attention getters for that thesis. They read examples of a startling statement, a quotation, an anecdote, and a question for the same thesis. They look at the term *anecdote* and read "Bob goes

from getting an F on his first essay in Miss Webster's English class to an A on the second essay. What caused such a drastic change?" or they look at the term *quotation* and read "Fender asserts that 'Love is not blind, but it is a curtain of stupidity.'"

- For the young writers to recognize the variety of attention getters, they read various attention getters and label each one as a startling statement, a quotation, an anecdote or very short story, and a question. For example, they label "Two-thirds of the students in this class will fail because they do not do their weekly assignments" as a startling statistic and they label "What can students do to succeed in a writing class?" as a question. They label their own attention getter.

- When students are given a thesis, they can be asked to write an attention getter as a startling statement, a quotation, an anecdote or very short story, or a question. As they practice with the thesis of "Having a car results in many negative experiences," they write each type of attention getter for this thesis and then select the one that is the most exciting.

- Within a small group of students with this same learning gap, they write an attention getter for a given topic. These students share their attention getters with each other by identifying the type and identifying the degree of interest. The others give their opinion and provide suggestions for improving these attention getters.

- Often pupils have no idea what to write in their attention getter. One strategy is for them to take the topic up to a broader level. Their topic can fit under the umbrella of several different bigger topics. For example, "TV programs" is a subtopic of "entertainment," "TV," "relaxation," "viewers," or "programming" (Figure 8.26). Visual students like creating a bubble map in which their thesis topic is the initial bubble and the higher bubbles indicate the bigger topics. The writers can then write attention getters about these bigger topics.

- Certain writers write a good attention getter but lack a bridge to the actual thesis. They may state, "Within the next three hours, eighty people will die from cancer." They have a great startling statement. However, their thesis, "People should walk to be physically fit" does not provide a logical connection between the attention getter and the thesis. They can use the strategy of adding a statement to bridge the attention getter and the thesis, such as "The chances of cancer are drastically reduced when a person is physically fit." Therefore the introductory paragraph becomes, "Within the next three hours, eighty people will die from cancer. The chances of getting cancer are drastically reduced when a person is physically fit. People should walk to be physically fit." Students can ask themselves, "Does my attention getter naturally flow into the thesis or do I need to add a bridge?"

**Figure 8.26 Attention Getter Going Up From the Topic**

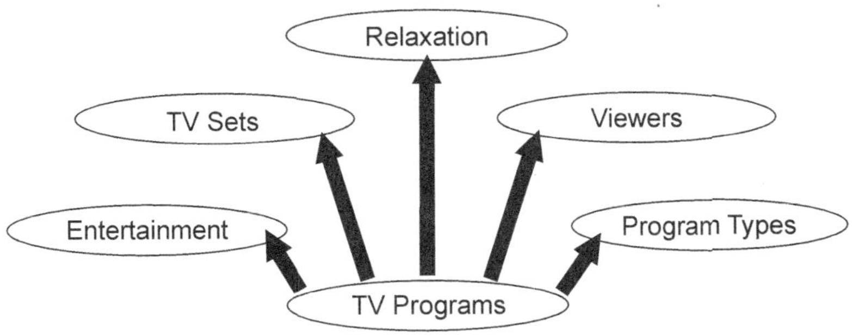


- When learners transition to academic essay writing, they often carry over many of the literary writing ideas about an introduction. For example, one student writes a three-quarter page introduction to a two-page essay. Literary introductions tend to be much longer as these introductions set up a story. Academic essay writing does not use such lengthy introductions as the "meat" of an academic essay consists of the body paragraphs. These scribes can ask themselves "Does my introduction give away the 'meat' of my writing? A movie trailer may show all the important parts of a movie so there is no reason to see the movie. Is there a reason to read the rest of my essay after reading the introduction?"
- You suggest a sentence limit for the introductory paragraph to force students to limit themselves to the attention getter and the thesis. One teacher asserts that the introductory paragraph is only 5% of the total essay or just over four word-processed lines; if there are sixty-six lines in a two-page essay, 5% is 3.3 lines for the introduction. If you decide that the introductory paragraph is 10% of the total essay, the students' introduction will only be 6.6 word-processed lines. The reality of these numbers shocks students into changing their writing. They have the goal of writing the introductory paragraph with an attention getter and the thesis in 6.6 lines. A quick count of their lines can determine if they have kept their writing tightly to the attention getter and the thesis.
- Students benefit from seeing a long, wandering introduction being transformed into one that only has the attention getter and the thesis statement. They can watch a teacher or student-made Power Point presentation and ask the students, "Is this an attention getter?" and "Is this the thesis?" as you eliminate many of the sentences. As you look at "How do people cool down in the summer? Some people prefer to go someplace like the mountains. The mornings are refreshing. The heat of the summer makes people want to find wet places so they can cool down. Going to the pool differs from going to the beach. There are many beautiful beaches in our area. The most popular one is Beaver Lake but I never go there," you realize that

the thesis should be the last sentence in an introductory paragraph, so you eliminate any sentences after the thesis statement that do not help with the thesis. Therefore you eliminate "There are many beautiful beaches in our area. The most popular one is Beaver Lake but I never go there."

- For strategies on developing the thesis, please review the Thesis section (see page 65).

## Feedback

Changing from literary and self-expressive introductions to academic writing introductions presents a challenge to many students. Students benefit from being told when they are writing in a narrative mode instead of an academic one. Also, they grow from learning new ways of writing when their old way is ineffective. When students try a new strategy, you encourage them since trying a new strategy involves the students moving from a comfort zone to a risk zone. For example, you may offer comments like "Remember that I'm here to help you whenever you want help" or "I like it when you ask me questions because I know that you are thinking."

## Time to Grow

The best time for growth occurs immediately after the students have written their introductory paragraph and someone has assessed that paragraph. The growth takes place through a variety of strategies that directly help the students start to overcome their learning gap. You will include time for the students to practice this new strategy in class and to receive instant feedback. Students show their growth in writing an introductory paragraph by labeling their confidence level using a 1 to 4 scale where 4 = very confident, 3 = fairly confident, 2 = beginning to feel confident, and 1 = not confident.

## Reporting Growth

When writers begin doing academic writing, they still tend to employ the long introductory paragraph mentality. As they change to the academic writing, they notice that their introductions become drastically shorter. One student changed from a meandering twenty-line introduction to a six-line introduction that precisely presented the attention getter and the thesis. You may want students to keep track of the number of sentences in their first academic essay introduction and the numbers on subsequent ones so they can visualize their growth.

You can post the students' exemplary introductory paragraphs on a class "Wall of Great Writers." Students are proud of their writing achievement when they view their introductory paragraphs on the wall. Although students may not have their first introductory paragraphs on the wall, they will beam with pride as they improve and their exemplar introductory paragraphs are posted.

# Concluding Paragraph

## Information

Students who struggle with concluding paragraphs express themselves in sentences such as the following:

- ♦ I wasn't sure what went in a conclusion.
- ♦ I'm used to writing very long conclusions; it was hard to switch to concise ones.
- ♦ A little hard to summarize the key points in short sentences or phrases.
- ♦ My conclusions tend to go in a direction far from the thesis.

Students become discouraged when they are not sure what they are to do, when they do not know how to do something, and when they are unsure if they have done it correctly. In formative assessment, you clearly state the learning goal, make sure the students understand it, model the learning through think alouds and exemplars, scaffold the learning, and gives constant feedback for growth. Formative assessment focuses on small wins so that students can be successful.

A student thinks of a concluding paragraph as saying goodbye to her grandmother as she leaves from a week visit. She thinks of all the good times they had during this visit; she summarizes the visit in her mind. Another student has the mental image of a concluding paragraph like a boss who wants to know whether the worker did what he was supposed to during his shift.

## Monitor

Learners, a peer, or you can label the three parts of the concluding paragraph. They write *thesis* for a paraphrase of the thesis, *categories* for a brief statement of the major categories used to prove the thesis, and *extender* for extending the topic idea or providing an additional insight into the topic.

## Diagnosis

### *Identify the Students' Learning Strength or Gap*

When students have a concluding paragraph with all three parts and each part fully serves its purpose, they demonstrate the strength of being able to write a concluding paragraph. However, when they do not have a concluding paragraph, are missing any of the three parts, or each part does not fully serve its purpose, they have a learning gap.

### *Identify Strategies to Overcome That Gap*

- ♦ Because struggling writers often do not understand what constitutes a concluding paragraph, they read many examples and identify all the parts in each paragraph. To create this material, you go to the digital file of exemplary past students' essays and pull out the concluding paragraphs. Then you can take these exemplary concluding paragraphs, create a copy, and label each part in these paragraphs. You give the concluding paragraphs to the students to identify the parts and make the copy with the labeled parts available as an answer key.

- These young learners read examples of several categories of extenders such as quotation ("Writing purifies the soul and the world"), future/consequence/result ("Students are now ready to impress their bosses with their new writing skills"), call to action ("Students can use their new writing skills to solve critical world issues"), and answering a question posed in the attention getter ("Good writers are remembered for their writing skills"). They then label the type of extender used in the provided sentences, verifying their answers with a paper or digital answer key. The pupils label their own extender or create one in one of these styles.
- Within a small group of pupils who share this learning gap, the learners can collectively brainstorm various extenders for a thesis. They may want to use the "go big" concept of expanding the topic. They think of all the topics that this topic is a part of and then write an extender based on that. For example, for the topic of "parties," they may extend the topic out to "fun," "weekends," "dancing," and "friends"; they select "weekends" and write "Parties are just one way of having fun on the weekend. Increase the fun factor by doing other things."
- These young scribes can improve in writing the first sentence of the concluding paragraph by rewriting the thesis from the introductory paragraph. They can use synonyms for the key elements of the thesis to express the same idea in a slightly different manner.
- Some students may learn best through a watching a video or online slide show on concluding paragraphs. You may record your think aloud about writing a concluding paragraph so that students can review it at any time and any place. Students who have already demonstrated success at writing concluding paragraphs can create an e-movie or Power Point to explain to others how to be successful. After watching, those learners with the learning gap read an essay that is missing a concluding paragraph and they write a concluding paragraph. Then they read several possible concluding paragraphs and compare those to their paragraph.

## Feedback

You avoid giving vague feedback such as "Please improve your concluding paragraph"; "Work more on this"; "Refocus the paragraph"; or "Rewrite." Instead you provide feedback as to what the exact learning gap is and what specific strategy will cause an improvement. Before you suggest the strategy to the students, you ask, "Will this strategy lead directly to an improvement?" and "How does this strategy match the students' preferred learning style?"

## Time to Grow

The class time just after learning of the concluding paragraph gap is the best time for growth. Students can practice the new strategy in class and have peers or you assure them that they have overcome the learning gap. If they have not improved, then they receive a different strategy as an alternative route to success.

## Reporting Growth

Students, a peer, or you can put a plus sign (+) in front of each part of the concluding paragraph that shows a strength. When the writers see these three plus signs, they know that they have grown in this skill.

You allow the students class time to email or text their parents to tell them that they now can write a successful concluding paragraph.

# 9

# Writing Process: Revise

The revision part of the writing process traditionally includes the students, peers, or you assessing the writing draft and then the students improving their writing (Figure 9.1). However, in the formative assessment process, almost all aspects of their writing have already been assessed and improved before the learners reach this part (Figure 9.2). In formative assessment, as writers go from the draft to their final version, they make minimal changes.

**Figure 9.1. The Role of Revision in Formative Assessment**

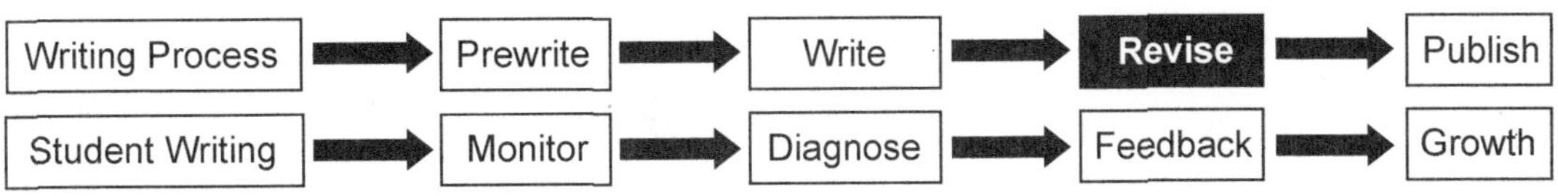


**Figure 9.2. Writing and Revising**

This section includes:

- "I can" statements
- Checklist
- Essay Improvement

## "I can" Statements

### Information

Students comment that they become confused during the writing process when they write as follows:

- I get lost in what I'm to do.
- I leave out a part because I forget about it.
- Help!

When you use a formative assessment approach in class, your young writers can always tell where they are in the process and where they have to be in terms of their writing. They know what skills they need to use to be successful. Unfortunately, most writing standards or learning goals do not identify the major points along the learning journey. "I can" statements identify the many steps involved in a learning goal journey; if students perform all of these steps, they will be successful (Figure 9.3). Because these statements are written in terms of what the student can do, they are called "I can" statements. Figure 9.4 illustrates a partial "I can" listing for an argument research paper.

**Figure 9.3. I Can and Success**

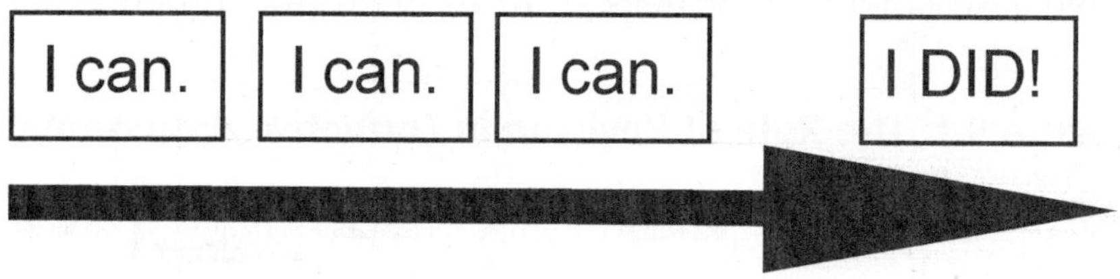


**Figure 9.4. Argument Research Paper Partial "I can" Statements**

I can

___ Select or create a debatable topic that I will use to persuade my readers.

___ Limit the topic so that I can prove my point in three pages.

___ Brainstorm many ideas about the topic.

___ Evaluate my ideas using 3 (high), 2 (medium), 1 (low) and modify or delete my low quality ideas.

___ Organize my ideas into categories.

___ Create a graphic organizer, outline, or concept map of all that I presently know about the topic.

___ Identify what additional categories I will need.

___ Identify the opposing points of view about my topic and figure out how to disprove these in my paper.

___ Select specific reference information from reliable sources that directly proves my point.

___ Copy down the full citation for each reference.

___ Decide whether to paraphrase the source information or to quote a very short passage of the information.

A learner compares "I do" statements to her own person "to-do" list. Her list helps her to make sure she gets done what she needs to each day. Another person imagines "I can" statements as the mapping program on his father's cell phone that tells him each driving turn to take to arrive at the destination.

## Monitoring

The scribes check off each learning skill on the "I can" sheet as they do them. Students, a peer, or you can use these statements to measure progress through the writing process. You may look over this "I can" skills list to compare it to the students' actual writing at any stage; their lack of "I can" statements may represent a lack of understanding about this particular type of writing.

## Diagnosis

### *Identify the Students' Learning Strength or Gap*

When learners have checked off those "I can" statements that represent their writing progress, they have a strength in self-assessment. When students have checked their "I can" statements; they can visualize exactly how far they have moved in their writing from the beginning and they observe how far they have yet to go. By reading the unchecked "I can" statements, the pupils understand exactly what skills they will have to use as they continue in their writing. On the other hand, if students have not checked off items on the "I can" sheet and have not done those items, they have a major learning gap.

### *Identify Strategies to Overcome That Gap*

- Every other day throughout the writing unit, students take out their "I can" statements and assess where they are. You verify their statements to determine they have made progress.
- As you sit with a student, the student can check off items he or she has done. You may ask the student for evidence of doing the "I can" statement. Then you let the student know that you will be checking his or her list in a few days.
- You may have all students read the "I can" sheet and circle any learning skill that they do not understand. They hand these sheets in to you after you introduce the writing type. You meet individually with any student who does not understand the skills.

## Feedback

Students receive their own feedback as they check off the "I can" statements. When they look at these sheets every other day, they see what they have done. They see small steps leading to their success.

## Time to Grow

Because you build in-class time for the students to audit their "I can statements," they are constantly aware of what they have done and what they have yet to do. You may want students to write the dates of when they complete the "I can" statements so they can see their progress over a short period of time.

## Reporting Growth

A completed "I can" sheet represents a completed essay. Students feel a sense of satisfaction when they have checked off the last skill on the list. They can comprehend how far they have traveled in their writing. You may congratulate them with statements like "You successfully used many different writing skills in this essay!" and "Your high-quality essay shows that you carefully used all the skills!"

# Checklists

## Information

Learners may show a learning gap in using a writing checklist when they state:

- I've done it (the essay), I don't need to check it.
- I know it's good.
- I've made enough changes, I don't want to make any more.

Formative assessment checklists assist the students in assessing their own work (Figure 9.5). Because these checklists state specific skills, the students can verify for themselves that they have displayed this skill in their writing. In addition, peers or you can use the checklist to assess the writing.

**Figure 9.5. Classification Essay Checklist**

**Classification Writing**

______ Do I have an introduction?

______ Do I tell the topic and its categories in the thesis statement?

______ Do I have three different categories?

______ Do I make sure that the categories do not overlap?

______ Do I arrange the categories in a logical order?

______ Do I provide a definition and an example of each category?

______ Do I have four different characteristics that I use in each category paragraph?

______ Do I position the four different characteristics in the same order in each paragraph?

_______ Do I supply specific details to explain each category?

_______ Do I use transition words to guide the reader through the paper?

_______ Do I use mechanics (correct sentence structure, grammar, etc.) to communicate my ideas?

_______ Do I use precise vocabulary?

_______ Do I have a conclusion?

A student compares a writing checklist to his mother's grocery list. She makes sure that she has all the things on the list by checking them off as she puts them in the chart. Another student thinks of a checklist as using a list to get ready for party. By checking the list, he knows he has everything he needs for the party.

## Monitoring

The students, a peer or you can check to see if the skills are checked off the writing checklist. Likewise, the students, a peer or you can confirm that those skills are in the students' writing by writing the number of the skill next to its location in the writing.

## Diagnosis

### *Identify the Students' Learning Strength or Gap*

When students have checked off items on their writing checklist and those skills appear in their writing, then they have a strength in self-assessing with a checklist. Conversely, if students have not checked off the skills or have checked off skills that do not appear in their writing, then they have a learning gap in using a writing checklist. Sometime the student checks off each skill such as those in Figure 9.5 as being present, but the student does not actually demonstrate the skills in the writing.

### *Identify Strategies to Overcome That Gap*

- One technique that can help these struggling students to focus on the checklist is a line-numbering technique. The students print out their paper and number each line. When they check items off the list, they add the line number in which the checklist item appears. So for item 2, "Do I tell the topic and its categories in the thesis statement?" the student checks it off and then writes the line number from the paper for the thesis:

  √ Line 4 2. Do I tell the topic and its categories in the thesis statement?

- Another technique is for the students to write in the number of the checklist skill where the skill appears in the word-processed document. For example, they may write "Students should not be required to take a World Language (2)" with the number two indicating the checklist item for number two, the thesis.

- ♦ You ask some students about the gap. One student shares, "I know I have to do it so I just put down checks. I'm too tired after writing the essay to think any more." You decide that you will have all students do their checklist in class and revise their essay in class. By giving them in-class time, you are ensuring a higher level of writing.
- ♦ If students do not seem able to identify the skills in their writing, you have them read a checklist and a sample essay in which you have labeled each skill. Next, they are to apply the checklist to a sample paragraph, label each skill, and then check an answer key. Then, the learners can apply the checklist to an essay and again check an answer key. Finally, they can apply the checklist to their own writing.
- ♦ If students display the learning gap of simply checking all the skills when these skills are not present in their writing, they can meet one-on-one with you as you guide them through the checklist and their own paper.

## Feedback

When students do the checklist and have those skills in their writing, you can acknowledge their success with statements like, "Your checklist accurately reflects your writing skills" and "You have self-assessed what you have included in your writing through a writing checklist and made changes to improve your writing. Good work!"

## Time to Grow

As you plan out your class, you include in-class time just after the learners have written their draft for them to assess their writing using the writing checklist and for them to make their revisions. Twenty minutes of class time will result in the students making significant changes to their writing. If students plan on doing the writing checklist and revisions at home, they are less likely to do the checklist and much less likely to make any revisions.

## Reporting Growth

As your students self-check themselves using a writing checklist and make subsequent improvements in their paper, they realize that they are empowered to improve themselves. They feel their ability to grow in their writing by carefully applying the checklist to their papers. Likewise, as you assess their papers, you notice the changes between the draft and the final paper that are due to their applying the checklist. You congratulate them with a statement like, "I've noticed that you have used the checklist to make major improvements to your work."

# Essay Improvement Sheet

## Information

Students reveal that improving from essay to essay can be difficult in words such as the following:

- I seem to have the same problems in each essay.
- I'm not getting any better.
- Topic sentences still cause me difficulties.

Your goal for the students is for them to grow in their ability to write and not to stagnate. Formative assessment affirms that the pupils are to be aware of their learning gaps and overcome those gaps. They should not constantly repeat the same ineffective writing. With each essay they grow.

A student compares this essay improvement sheet to her baseball game stats. Each time she tries to do better than the last game, in terms of getting more runs and catching more balls. Another student thinks of the essay improvement sheet like a personal best screen in his video game.

You decide to use an essay improvement chart form (Figure 9.6) for the students to record their major learning gaps and their improvements from essay to essay. When you return their first writing and the rubric to the students, they make a three-column chart. The first column is "essay type," the second "feedback," and the third "improvements." In the first column, the students write down the essay type that they just received back such as "cause and effect." In the second column, they copy the two or three feedback comments from the rubric that you think are the most crucial for improvement. In the third column, they tell what change they made and, more importantly, they include examples from their new essay. Their new examples demonstrate that they have incorporated the suggested changes.

**Figure 9.6. Essay Improvement**

| Essay Type | Teacher Feedback | My Improvements in the New Essay |
|---|---|---|
| Cause and Effect | 1. Use a topic sentence in each body paragraph.<br>2. Give details for each piece of evidence.<br>3. Shorten and focus your attention grabber. | 1. Now I start each paragraph with a topic sentence which included the thesis and the category. My example: "Youth violence can be reduced by not allowing young people to play violent video games."<br>2. Now I use specific numbers, dates, or amounts instead of general statements. My example: "In the game 'Shoot'em,' the average player kills two hundred people."<br>3. Now, instead of writing a long story (many paragraphs) for an attention grabber, I write a mini-story of several sentences that ties to the topic. My example: "A recent news story reported that a nine-year-old boy wanted to do in real life what he did in his video game. He got his father's pistol and shot his brother who died instantly." |
| Contrast | | |

## Monitoring

You can verify that students have written your formative feedback into their essay improvement sheet. Likewise, you can affirm that they have included the specific change they have made and that they have an example from the new essay that illustrates that change. In a formative assessment mentality, you ask for the essay improvement sheet at the time of the draft to confirm that students have made the improvements.

## Diagnosis

### *Identify the Students' Learning Strength or Gap*

If students have responded to the formative feedback and have included a specific change and its example from the new essay, then they are proficient at improving from essay to essay. Conversely, if they have not listed your formative feedback, do not indicate the specific change, and do not supply an example, or if the example does not illustrate the change, then they have a learning gap in improving from essay to essay.

### *Identify Strategies to Overcome That Gap*

- Students with this learning gap benefit from copying the two or three critical feedback statements into the essay improvement chart as soon as they receive back the essay. The act of copying it reinforces that they do have a learning gap and that they can improve. If students are confused, you can have them insert a question mark next to the teacher feedback statement they don't understand and then indicate exactly what they do not understand about the feedback suggestion on how to become better. They hand the sheet in to you.
- If pupils cannot identify what they are to do to improve in this skill, then they cannot improve. They may need to take your formative assessment suggestions and highlight the special change such as "be more concrete in your details—use the facts of *numbers, specific places, and precise actions.*" You may ask them to write a specific number, place and action to verify that they understand the specificity required such as "twenty miles" or "Helen's Hut in Rochester." Then they can make some imprecise details in their essay precise. Next they can rewrite a sentence or two from the present essay to demonstrate their use of details.
- Students can confirm that their examples show the change by comparing their work to an exemplar. They compare their newly written topic sentences to the exemplar's topic sentences. They underline the topic and double underline the controlling idea in the topic sentences in the exemplar and in their essay. The learners may compare the two.

## Feedback

When students show you that they have been able to make the change from a learning gap to a strength, you can congratulate them with statements such as, "Congratulations, you can write topic sentences! " or "Your writing shows that you know the difference between an effective topic sentence and an ineffective one." If you find that they have not grown from essay to another, then you will want to work one-on-one or in a small group of students with the same learning gap.

## Time to Grow

The time just after receiving the essay with your formative feedback on the rubric is the golden time for students to copy their formative feedback to their improvement sheet, to practice the improvement, and to begin making the improvements. You may build in the "three most common problems in your last essay" time immediately after the return of each essay to help students while the learning gap is still fresh in their minds. In addition, you have the formative activities ready for the various groupings so that they can learn how to overcome the reoccurring gap.

## Reporting Growth

Students can monitor their own growth by looking at their essay improvement sheet. As they notice the different formative assessment concerns each essay, they realize that they are not repeating the same gaps. Furthermore, they realize their formative feedback changes from identifying major problems (lack of a thesis) to identifying minor problems (a comma problem) as they grow in their writing skill. Teachers can celebrate the students' growth from essay to essay with statements such as, "You've certainly have shown that you can write an introductory paragraph now when you could not in the last essay" or "Great improvement. You've overcome your problem of not including details!"

# 10

# Conclusion

Your students have gone through the writing process with the formative assessment approach. They have changed from struggling to successful writers. They can publish their proficient work to the class "Wall of Fame," the class website or wiki, a district-wide writing wiki, or a multischool wiki.

Each time the students, peers or you formatively assess the students' writing by monitoring, diagnosing, giving feedback and providing time for growth, you guarantee writing mini-wins. The students accumulate the trophies of success for each small part of the writing process. Those small wins add to the learners' dramatic success (Figure 10.1). Students, you, and their parents can see the vast difference between the present essay and a previous essay.

**Figure 10.1. Formative Assessment Leads to Success**

You may wonder about the time management in implementing formative assessment. Each moment that you spend in formative assessment helps your students to overcome their major learning gaps translates into your pupils writing successfully sooner and more often. When your writers no longer repeat the same critical learning gap but move forward in their writing, their writing reaches a higher level. Likewise, as you use formative assessment at each stage of writing, you know that you will spend less time in repeating the same feedback because your students will overcome each learning gap as it appears. You help your students to be better at peer-assessing and self-assessing for critical aspects of writing so that they can help others and themselves improve so that you do not have to look at each step within each part of the writing process. Instead of spending major time at the usual revision stage of writing, you redistribute this time in the earlier stages of writing in formative assessment.

You may want to start by implementing one aspect of formative assessment at a time, such as the prerequisites of unpacking the standards, deciding on assessments, or obtaining exemplars. Then you can practice your monitoring skills. Next, develop your skills in diagnosis. From diagnosis, you can move on to giving feedback. Subsequently, you can plan your class time to allow for in-class growth time. By developing each skill individually, you can be sure that you have the foundation for the next skill (Figure

10.2). You can test out your skill to be sure that you are proficient at it before using it. At any time, you can review the chapters in this book to guide you to be more successful. You use the same formative assessment procedure that you want your students to use to become better writers.

**Figure 10.2. Adding Formative Assessment Skills**

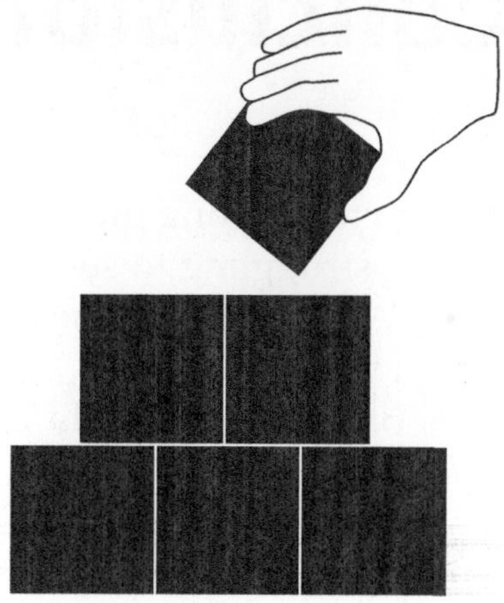

Add One Formative Assessment Skill at a Time

Through your use of formative assessment, your students will show great gains in writing in a relatively short time period.

As you begin to implement formative assessment, you might want to be aware of some possible pitfalls. If you have not precisely defined what the proficient level is for each aspect of writing, then you or your students will not be able to tell if they have reached that level. Also, you may find it hard to limit yourself to three pieces of feedback and to avoid the tendency to "red pen" their writing. Likewise, it make take you awhile to learn to give targeted feedback that will lead directly to your students' growth. Allow yourself time to build up your bank of strategy feedback; as you suggest new strategies, add them to your bank. Furthermore, you may find that you want to practice using specific phrases to invite students to change instead of the usual phrases of telling them to change. Additionally, you may have to turn your monitoring radar on high so you constantly monitor essential learning in your classroom on a daily basis. A last pitfall is that you may find yourself changing from complaining about the lack of student progress to bragging about the constant improvement of the students.

# References

## Works Cited

Ainsworth, L., & Viegut, D. (2006). *Common Formative Assessments*. Thousand Oaks, CA: Corwin Press.

Brookhart, S. M. (2008). *How to Give Effective Feedback to Your Students*. Alexandria, VA: Association for Supervision and Curriculum Development.

Bender, J. M. (2007). *The Resourceful Writing Teacher: A Handbook of Essential Skills and Strategies*. Portsmouth, NH: Heinemann.

Howell, R., Patton, S., & Deoitte, M. (2008). *Understanding Response to Intervention: A Practical Approach to Systemic Implementation*. Bloomington, IL: Solution Tree.

Hunter, M. (1976). Teacher Competency: Problem, theory and practice. *Theory Into Practice, 15*(2), 162–171.

Marzano, R. J. (2004). *Building Background Knowledge for Academic Achievement*. Alexandria, VA: Association for Supervision and Curriculum Development.

Silver, H. F., Strong, R. W., and Perini, M. J. (2007). *The Strategic Teacher: Selecting the Right Research-Based Strategy for Every Lesson*. Upper Saddle River, NJ: Pearson Education.

Tuttle, H. G. (2009). *Formative Assessment: Responding to Your Students*. Larchmont, NY: Eye On Education.

Wiggins, G. (1998). *Educative Assessment: Designing Assessments to Inform and Improve Student Performance*. San Francisco: Jossey-Bass.

## Bibliography

Black, P., & Wiliam, D. (1998). Inside the black box: Raising standards through classroom assessment. *Phi Delta Kappan, 80*(2), 139–148.

Benjamin, A. (2008). *Formative Assessment for English Language Arts*. Larchmont, NY: Eye On Education.

Calkins, L. M. (1986). *Art of Teaching Writing*. Portsmouth, NH: Heinemann.

Clarke, S. (2005). *Formative Assessment in Action: Weaving the Elements Together*. London: Hodder-Murray.

Hall, K., & Burke, W. M. (2003). *Making Formative Assessment Work: Effective Practice in the Primary Classroom*. Berkshire, UK: Open University Press.

Heritage, M. (2007). Formative assessment: What do teachers need to know and do? *Phi Delta Kappan, 89*(2), 140–145.

Marzano, R. J. (2000). *Transforming Classroom Grading*. Alexandria, VA: Association for Supervision and Curriculum Development.

Marzano, R. J. (2007). *The Art and Science of Teaching*. Alexandria, VA: Association for Supervision and Curriculum Development.

Popham, W. J. (2008). *Transformative Assessment*. Alexandria, VA: Association for Supervision and Curriculum Development.

Stiggins, R. J. (2007). *An Introduction to Student-Involved Assessment for Learning, 5th ed*. Upper Saddle River, NJ: Pearson Education.

Tuttle, H. G. (1994). *Restructuring Education for Quality Learning: From Ideas to Action*. Ithaca, NY: Epilog Visions.

## Online Sources

MY Access! (http://www.vantagelearning.com/school/products/myaccess/features.html)

Blackboard (http://www.blackboard.com/)

English-hilfen.de (http://www.englisch-hilfen.de/en/words/opposites2.htm)

Google Docs (http://docs.google.com)

Harry Tuttle's Education with Technology blog (http://www.eduwithtechn.wordpress.com)

Pearson's Intelligent Essay Assessor (http://www.pearsonkt.com/prodIEA.shtml)

Pbworks (http://pbworks.com)

Rubistar (http://rubistar.4teachers.org/)

Smartthinking.com (http://www.smarthinking.com/)

Thesaurus.com (http://thesaurus.reference.com)

Webspiration (http://www.mywebspiration.com)

Zoomerang (http://www.zoomerang.com)

9781596671287